W9-AHI-459

Advance Praise for *Not by Chance*

"Over the course of my career I have had dozens of parents seeking residential treatment say, "You know, it's not like there's a book on the process—we're learning as we go!" Now there is a book. Not by Chance *is a highly usable culmination of a career's worth of knowledge. Funny how a $25 book could be the factor that makes a several thousand dollar treatment process actually stick."*

—TONY MOSIER, LMFT, co-founder Telos RTC

"Tim Thayne's new work is a terrific read and a top rank guide to helping troubled adolescents and their families. Tim's observations are clinically unimpeachable and his worldly insights are unfailingly enlightening. Read this book if you are the parent of a troubled adolescent, but read it too if you just want to learn about relationships and life. Excellent."

—SCOTT JOHNSON, PH.D., former president American Association of Marriage and Family Therapy, director of Marriage and Family Therapy Ph.D. Program at Virginia Tech

"The transition from intensive treatment settings to the lesser structure of home community is a vital component in any treatment process. Tim Thayne's excellent book is a wonderful resource for families and professionals alike who are serious about retaining positive treatment gains while extending supportive scaffolding to ensure long-term success. Tim's pioneering work with hundreds of clients over many years allows the reader to know that what is shared comes from careful research, personal experience and verified success. I highly recommend Not by Chance.*"*

—KIMBALL DELAMARE, LCSW, founding president National Association of Therapeutic Schools and Programs

"After knowing Tim Thayne for 20 years, I can honestly say there isn't a better source of knowledge, information and wisdom on how to lead a healthy, worthy life at home and in your family. He knows what to do to bring a special-needs or troubled teen and their family to a wonderful position of interaction, growth and maturity."

—DR. HAROLD KURSTEDT, Hal G. Prillaman Emeritus
Professor, Virginia Tech, co-founder Newport Group

"Not by Chance *is intriguing, pragmatic and honest. In it, Dr. Thayne takes a refreshingly practical focus on the critical points where the-rubber-meets-the-road in terms of a parent's role in out-of-home treatment for teenagers. He draws on his extensive experience as an adolescent therapist and parent coach to spell out how positive change becomes habit. This should be required reading for every family who places their adolescent in a residential treatment program."

—DR. NICOLAS TAYLOR, psychologist, author of *Helping People Addicted to Methamphetamine: A Creative New Approach for Families and Communities*

"Our son attended boarding school for eighteen months and I only wish we had had the guidance Tim Thayne has shared with such good cheer and candor. The book is an absorbing, empathetic guide to the hazards that families can and will experience when welcoming a teen home from an extended stay away. His explanations about what to expect and do are enlightening and inspiring. Any parent prepared with his guidance will be better able to ensure that the growth their teen has made will be sustainable."

—ALYSON VON FELDT, co-author of *Running into the Wind: Bronco Mendenhall, Five Strategies for Building a Successful Team*, co-founder Crimson Corporation

"Dr. Thayne has provided the compass for many of my clients to successfully navigate the complex task of bringing their loved one home after treatment. Families who have worked with Tim report that they could not have enjoyed the same successes without taking this step. After observing these family's achievements first hand, I am more convinced than ever that the extended and integrative transitional support he offers is a critical component for lasting change."

—SARAH FINNEY, LMFT, Educational Consulting Services

"Dr. Tim Thayne has provided vital information, examples, principles and ideas that help support parents of troubled teens. We need all the help we can find in order to see our children become moral, independent and happy. I'm grateful for the opportunity to support the fine work in this book. With its teachings—and our best efforts—clear and real success is within reach!"

—DERRY L. BRINLEY, M.D., child and adolescent psychiatrist, co-author of *The Balanced Life*

"I believe Not by Chance *could be considered a general parenting book, in addition to helping those with troubled teens. What most of us struggle with in change is figuring out how to make it sustainable. Archimedes said, 'Give me a lever long enough, a fulcrum strong enough, and I'll move the world.'" What Dr. Thayne has done in this book is define the levers that will enable each of us to change our context, behaviors, and ultimately our little corner of the world…our homes."*

—KENDALL LYMAN, co-author of *The Employee Engagement Mindset,* principal of The Cornerstone Group

"I wish this book had been available a few years ago when one of our children entered a residential program. Tim Thayne's wise and seasoned counsel would have been such a blessing to us then. He deserves thanks for writing such a straightforward and plain-spoken guidebook for parents with challenging children. The stories and examples richly illustrate the principles taught, making them come alive and easy to understand. Dr. Thayne has given families everywhere a precious gift."

—SCOTT FARNSWORTH, president SunBridge, Inc., co-founder Main Street Philanthropy

"Go-to-Guide for parents on the brink of sending their child to residential treatment. How it works. Why it works. How you can get it to stick when you bring your child back home."

—ANNE LEWIS, NA, CEP, Educational and Therapeutic Placement Specialist

Not by Chance

Not by Chance

HOW PARENTS BOOST
THEIR TEEN'S SUCCESS
IN *and* AFTER TREATMENT

TIM R. THAYNE, Ph.D.

Co-author of *Taking the Reins*

Advantage®

Published by Advantage, Charleston, South Carolina.
Member of Advantage Media Group.

ADVANTAGE is a registered trademark and the Advantage colophon is a trademark of Advantage Media Group, Inc.

Printed in the United States of America.

ISBN: 978-1-59932-317-6
LCCN: 2013951878

10 9 8 7 6

This publication is designed to provide accurate and authoritative information in regard to the subject matter covered. It is sold with the understanding that the publisher is not engaged in rendering legal, accounting, or other professional services. If legal advice or other expert assistance is required, the services of a competent professional person should be sought.

Advantage Media Group is proud to be a part of the Tree Neutral® program. Tree Neutral offsets the number of trees consumed in the production and printing of this book by taking proactive steps such as planting trees in direct proportion to the number of trees used to print books. To learn more about Tree Neutral, please visit www.treeneutral.com. To learn more about Advantage's commitment to being a responsible steward of the environment, please visit www.advantagefamily.com/green

Advantage Media Group is a publisher of business, self-improvement, and professional development books and online learning. We help entrepreneurs, business leaders, and professionals share their Stories, Passion, and Knowledge to help others Learn & Grow. Do you have a manuscript or book idea that you would like us to consider for publishing? Please visit advantagefamily.com or call 1.866.775.1696.

CONTENTS

ACKNOWLEDGMENTS

LET ME START BY thanking my wife, Roxanne. We have five children, but this book counts as our sixth baby together. The 22-year incubation and countless 4 a.m. feedings have resulted in the birth of a work we hope will bless the lives of families and homes everywhere. Her involvement in my life and work began in graduate school and stretches into every aspect of the office, farm and home today. It takes a special person to be in such constant contact with me and make me feel that she loves it. Thank you to my sons and daughter, who have an expert father who ought to read his own book sometimes.

A special thanks to Dr. Bryan Zitzman, whose gift for detail, ability to bring a team together, superhuman stamina and loyalty have made him the best hire I've ever made. To Dawnie Williams, whose brains and cheerful "You bet" make me feel that all things are possible with her to track, organize, and balance me.

To all of the current and past Homeward Bound coaches and staff for their creative and personal contributions to our curriculum, experience and success in homes everywhere.

To Lee Caldwell, Jason Adams, Mary Alexine, Tony Mosier, Paula Leslie, Tony Alonzo, Jenny Heckman, Shane Gallagher, Lucy Pritzker, Dan Stuart, Randy Oakley, Jared Balmer, Jon Worbets, Ken Newell, Kim Buczkowski and others who contributed to this work through interviews, focus groups and letters, please allow me to return the favor one day. To Rick Meeves, my long-time friend and partner for introducing me to this field. A broad and sincere thanks to all of the colleagues who encouraged me to address this gap in treatment. Warm gratitude goes to the families who allowed me to interview and share their stories of pain, growth and joy, that their experiences might go on to strengthen and inspire others. This work would fall flat without your cooperation, guidance and honesty.

A heartfelt thank you to members of the Brigham Young University Marriage and Family Therapy department who let me slide into their graduate program as an alternate and continue to aid me to this day. I hope you don't regret it. To my doctoral program professors at Virginia Tech, where innovation in research and practice was applauded; you put me on the road to an entrepreneurial career that I've loved. To Dr. Harold Kurstedt, as fine a man and mentor as I could have hoped for.

Thanks to the Advantage Media family for showing us how it's done, and especially to Jenny Tripp, who made us feel brilliant.

Lastly, a warm and deep gratitude is owed to the remarkable families who willingly open their front doors and hearts to us. Your courage and love inspires our mission.

FOREWORD

REMEMBER YOUR FIRST DAY of school? You may picture yourself clinging to a parent's hand and searching the classroom for a friendly face. Or think back to the day you left home for college or work, not knowing how the big wide world would receive or reward you. The anxiety it provoked was surely felt by both you and your parents.

By nature, transitions are difficult. They are difficult because they involve change—a potentially unsettling event. Sending a child to a therapeutic program, away from home, is one of the most difficult decisions a parent ever has to make. And one of the most difficult moves for the child. Add to that a second transition home again after completing the program and both scenarios are fraught with anticipatory anxiety for everyone: teens, parents, siblings, and treatment professionals alike

For an adolescent therapist like me, nothing is more exhilarating than seeing a family system change for the better. The likelihood of such a "new birth" is great if parent and child are fully engaged in the treatment process. Conversely, nothing is more devastating than witnessing parents who innocently—or knowing full well—undermine the process, confuse the teen, prolong the stay and ultimately botch the results. The significance of a parent's role during and following treatment cannot be overemphasized.

Historically, the transition home following an extended stay in therapeutic programs represented the Achilles heel of our mental health field. Far too often, therapeutic gains come unraveled on the bumpy road to full integration into the home environment. The old environment with all of its trappings can wreak havoc on the returnees and their caregivers. Fully aware of the hazards, many therapeutic programs have experimented with transition and aftercare services with varying levels of success. The less-than-stellar results lie, in part, in the fact that they do not rate as the highest priority of the treatment program staff—and rightfully so. Their number-one priority is treating the symptomatology that brought the child to the program in the first place.

This, however, is not the case for Dr. Tim Thayne. He has made a career out of creating and implementing a most successful formula for engaging moms and dads in an ideal parent/program partnership. Coaching parents and youth through the crucial weeks after discharge, to avoid major relapse, has been Dr. Thayne's top priority. Much like the pioneering Wright Brothers, he has spent well over a decade perfecting his "flying machine"—and it flies. Countless think-tank sessions, extensive reviews of the professional literature, experimentation and real-life testing have culminated in *Not by Chance.*

This work isn't only a book; it's an essential "parent manual." A manual is meant to be read and reread; referred to over and over again. This "pocket therapist" provides you with expert and concrete answers to questions and concerns that consistently arise while your child is away—and more importantly when he or she returns home again.

If you've ever thought, "So, what should I be doing while my teen is gone?" this book is exactly what you should be doing. I couldn't recommend that you spend your time in a more worthy pursuit.

—JARED U. BALMER, PHD

Founding Member, National Association of Therapeutic Schools and Programs (NATSAP)

Co-founder, Island View Residential Center, The Oakley School, and Aspen Institute for Behavioral Assessment, Co-founder/Owner WayPoint Academy

Huntsville, Utah 2013

The Worst Day
of My Career

I could see he was a handsome kid, even though his hair was bright green and he never smiled. Garrett had dyed his hair just before his parents sent him to us and his mom was convinced that he did so just because he knew that she loved his blond hair. It was only the latest way he'd found to demonstrate who was in charge. He was in full-fledged rebellion mode; whatever his parents wanted he was against. He was using drugs and alcohol and was regularly sneaking out at night. One of the brightest kids in his high school, he was failing most of his classes. His first week in our wilderness program, he was so angry that he wouldn't talk to me, and I didn't blame him. I would have been mad too.

It was December in Utah; there was over a foot of snow on the ground and Garrett was sleeping in a shelter of his own making, constructed with a single tarp stretched between trees with cordage. The second week, our staff pointed me in his direction, up a path that meandered into the trees. By the smiles on their faces, it was clear that the tension the staff had experienced just a week earlier, as they worried about Garrett doing something rash—like running—was gone.

As I walked toward Garrett's camp, I anticipated the familiar and welcome change in attitude we so often see after the initial anger has worn off: a softened expression, better eye contact, and a willingness to engage in conversation. My optimism for what I might find was founded upon the experiences I had had with so many other teens in the wilderness. Even though I'd seen it often, each time I witnessed that softening in attitude after the first difficult week, it was as if a small miracle had occurred in the life of that teen, and we would all feel joy because of it. But what I found that morning in the little clearing where he camped was a level of readiness, engagement and creativity that I'd never encountered before. Garrett had constructed a complete living room suite out of snow. He had a snow couch and coffee table. He had a little chair also made out of snow. He had a mat made from willows that he had placed on the couch for me to sit on to keep my posterior from getting wet, and he sat in his own chair eager to start our session.

That was the beginning of an amazing few weeks together in the wilderness as I witnessed Garrett's jolting hair color fade, his naturally happy disposition return and his drive to create and be productive manifest itself in the construction of dozens of primitive products: a backpack from willows and leather, a sling, a leather "possibles" bag, an assortment of eating utensils, a bullroarer (think of Crocodile Dundee), drums and a flute. From having been one of our toughest kids, Garrett had turned into a poster child for wilderness treatment. But, because I had seen too many failures with kids going home too quickly, when it was time for him to leave camp, I recommended to his parents that he go on to a therapeutic boarding school. They were directed by their educational consultant to a great coed, therapeutic-type boarding school, and I soon got word that he was considered one of their shining stars as well. I felt great about him, and his family. I'd gotten to know his father and mother quite well and chalked them up to being among my favorites. It seemed like a big win for all concerned.

We kept in touch, so I wasn't surprised in the least when I saw their number pop up on the phone's caller ID. I was expecting good news. But there was distress in Garrett's mother's voice and she was in tears.

She started to tell me the story of Garrett's return home and how he'd quickly reverted to some of his old negative behaviors: drinking, lying, sneaking out. I was devastated; this was the boy that I thought would surely be successful. We'd done all the things we felt would make the difference including the step-down therapeutic boarding school, and he'd gone home with the best recommendations the program therapist could give, with parents committed to outpatient therapy, substance abuse groups and family therapy. Yet none of it seemed to have helped, and again the family was plunged into crisis.

I literally caught the next plane to their home town to see him face to face. I was banking on the exceptional relationship we had established in the weeks spent together in the wilderness to give me special access to his heart and mind. If embers of lofty dreams for his future and love for his family were still aglow, my hope was to fan them into a fire that could be carefully tended to stay lit in the world he was now in.

When I arrived, his parents apologetically told me that Garrett had locked himself in his room and was refusing to see me. For his parents, their inability to get their son to do this simple thing—

to see me, someone who'd had an exceptional relationship with him—further defined their sense of failure as parents. For Garrett, the humiliation of facing someone who had seen him at his best, who had been there when his eyes were opened to the consequences of his poor choices, to his cherished family relationships and to his untapped potential, was too great. It was too much to have to face the great discrepancy between the path he had articulated for himself throughout his treatment experience and the destructive path he was back on.

Besides the overwhelming sense that they had failed as parents, they also began to question the whole process. At one point they asked me, "Tim, we did everything that you asked us to do and everything the next program asked of us. Why is this not working?" I did not have a good answer for them. They were loving, educated, engaged and willing, and they were faithfully following through with all of the things that had been asked of them.

Undoubtedly, the hardest day in my career was the one that I spent in their home, not having the answers for them, and being at a loss for how to help. Near dinner time and just before I needed to leave for the airport, Garrett decided to come out and talk to me for a minute. He would not look me in the eye, and I was unable to connect with him as I had before. After everything that had been worked through and sacrificed over the previous year, it was a crushing defeat—for him, for his parents, and for me.

On the plane home, I resolved that I would devote all my time to developing ways for parents and teens to make this transition successful. I never wanted to see another kid crash and burn while parents stood by, helpless. That notion was the birth of Homeward Bound. It meant stepping away from the successful endeavor I was part of and taking a big flier financially; but I knew it was the right thing to do. There was a gap in our understanding as professionals and it was causing kids to fail. Given what families had already been through, that was unacceptable.

Kids are not superhuman. They cannot always resist the incredibly strong pull of old habits, old temptations and old weaknesses. This was the realization I had in Garret's home in Portland. I wasn't alone in this revelation. At my first professional conference after starting Homeward Bound, colleagues would walk up to my little booth and say, "Aftercare ... whaaat? Weren't you just doing wilderness therapy?" When I explained that I wanted to work with the families in the home environment, nearly everyone was encouraging, happy to give me a big thumbs up and wish me luck with a "We'll be watching you, Tim. Let us know how it goes." Understandably, even when they clearly saw a need, they simply didn't have the time or energy to devote to it. They had their plates full just managing the progress of the teen in their care. All professionals have a unique focus or passion in their own field or practice—the transition to the home environment happens to be mine.

The Purposes of this Book

There are three driving reasons for why I have written the book you now hold in your hands.

1. **To educate you** on the vital role parents play throughout the treatment process and in the transition from treatment to home. That long-term success doesn't come about by chance, by hoping or simply because you shelled out a lot of money and sent your child away to get help. It requires work and change on your part, and it takes a concrete plan;

2. **To inspire you** to know how to get engaged immediately as a partner with your program of choice, and begin to make the changes now that tie directly to your teen's long-term success in the future;

3. **To coach you** on creating a doable concrete plan that when followed will maximize your teen's success and momentum following treatment.

Last summer we had an extended family reunion in Jackson Hole, Wyoming. Everyone, Grandma included, voted to participate in a white water rafting trip down the Snake River. Benson, our guide, was truly expert. He was cheerful, he was clear in his instructions, and he was confident where we were not. He consistently gave us plenty of warning before we hit the rapids. That forewarning and advice turned the experience from nerve racking to adventurous and fun. During slow times on the float, he made sure to point out the high water marks along the cliffs, or eagle's nests and grazing deer. He taught us about eddies and encouraged us, when it was safe, to jump in the river and splash around for fun. He passed out fleece jackets and hats to warm those who were shivering after being drenched in the spray. We were comforted by his presence and enjoyed the journey infinitely more than if we had just thrown our own raft in the river and tried to guess what was coming around the bend or what we were seeing.

Like Benson, I am here to serve as your guide. My team and I have run this river hundreds of times with families from every state and from countries abroad. I have learned where the rapids and waterfalls are and know how to prepare you and your teen for what's around the bend, so you know when to hold on tight, ride it out, paddle hard and fast to change course and when to sit back and enjoy the trip. This book is to help parents who are anxious find hope and peace. Conversely, it's also meant to encourage parents who are apathetic or in denial about the challenges that lie ahead to wake up and engage wholeheartedly.

Warnings aside, there is so much to be optimistic about. By deciding to get help and put your teen in the hands of a qualified, reputable program, you have proactively taken advantage of the professional wisdom, experience and nurturing environment created specifically for the challenges your son or daughter is facing. You love your child and you are willing to pay the emotional price of separation to allow the healing to begin. Your faith in the treatment process, and the love you have for your son or daughter, exemplified by your sacrifice, inspires me and tells me there is a lot to work with here.

When your treatment program and your teen's progress indicate that it's time for your teen to return to the natural environment of home and family, the baton is being passed back to you. Just as in a relay race, when the hand off of your teen comes, you don't want to be standing there either frozen in fear or confusion, or asleep at the wheel. Your goal is to be running ahead, looking back over your shoulder at the program, ready to connect firmly and making a smooth transition from treatment to home. There is no reason for a loss of the momentum due to lack of knowledge and a plan. I know you're probably thinking, "Tim, we are tired. We have worked with our child and her issues for years. We have gone the rounds with outpatient therapy, school administrators, prayer, well-intentioned parenting advice and sleepless nights. What on earth could you tell us that we don't already know? To be frank, we are sick to death of reading self-help books in which professionals tout the ABCs and 1-2-3s of parenting our special needs or troubled teen."

All I can say is congratulations. You, my friend, are my ideal reader. You love your teen dearly and you have invested in your teen's success with everything you have. And although you might be exhausted and doubt your ability to persevere through the challenges I'm alluding to, if you have hope—and that's what this book is designed to give you— you'll also have the energy required to finish the journey strong. Though your teen's issues and your family's journey may be unique, your experience with treatment and transition will not be. Sure, you can reinvent the wheel and go it alone, but my mission has been to create a concrete educational map for parents who don't want to leave the outcome to chance or to the unfiltered and unchanged influences of the world they will come back to. Creating this process is my passion. It doesn't have to be yours.

> As you read, keep a highlighter and a pad of sticky notes with you. Highlight whatever strikes a chord or needs to be shared.

Think of this book as your blueprint for putting together the most thought-out, research-based, and proven model available for your son's or daughter's successful transition between treatment and home, because that's exactly what it is. In these pages I have given you all the tools, advice and inspiration I've got to help you make the most of the treatment investment. In fact I can't think of anything else to do, short of physically coming into your home to coach you through every step or crisis. All in all, this book is the least expensive, most palatable and efficient vehicle for getting squarely into your hands the crucial information and tools your family's situation requires. As you read, keep a highlighter and a pad of sticky notes with you.

Highlight whatever strikes a chord or needs to be shared. Then slap a sticky note on the pages that you know you will be returning to again, and label with a key word or two. This book is meant to be marked, shared and reread.

I guarantee that if you stick with me through to the end of the book, by the time you get through all those dog-eared, highlighted and note-filled pages, you'll slam the book shut and declare, "Okay, let's get this show on the road!" I'm all yours.

All or Nothing:
What It Takes to Succeed

C raig was coming out of the front door as I was walking up the driveway. He carried two suitcases full of tools and computer equipment. He was wet with perspiration. As our IT guy, it had been his job to enter this beautiful California home and get it wired up and ready for the video coaching we were going to do with our first Homeward Bound family.

On entering the home, I looked up to see white video cable strung high on the living room wall, leading down the hall to be plugged into the kitchen desktop computer. The anxious parents greeted me at the door, evidently willing to do whatever it took for me to help them with their daughter's return from a year of residential treatment.

In our Marriage and Family Therapy graduate program, videotaping our sessions was a powerful tool that produced rapid understanding and paved the way for a fledgling therapist's faster growth. Just as teens can become defensive when therapists tell them what they observed in their behavior, parents will often do the same thing when a therapist tries to help them recognize their contributions to negative patterns their teen exhibits. But *showing* them a playback of their voices raised, their teen's eyes rolling, their waffling and uncertainty about boundaries is a completely different ball game. There is little room for subjectivity and not much need for coaching. The information is in living color, right there for them to soak in and understand for themselves.

Knowing this, I decided to use videotaping in the work we would do for Homeward Bound families. Things were set up, with the family's permission of course, so that I could sit at my desk in my office and pan and zoom around the living room. The family was instructed to go into the room when they were going to discuss a subject that would bring up powerful feelings, or when there was an argument going on. I could then immediately and precisely coach them as they used new communication skills to navigate the crisis. Later, the family could access a playback of the digital recording as a refresher course if they needed it.

And it worked. A parent from Miami watched himself on video as he addressed a drinking incident with his daughter. His weak attempt to implement preset consequences for her actions summoned this response from him in our coaching session: "That was the most pitiful display of parenting I've ever seen. I will never do that again." I didn't need to say a word. He could see it all on his own. Another parent from Connecticut said, "If you think you know about your relationships with your kids and spouse, there is no substitute for seeing the experience live. For me, the video feedback was eye opening and revealing. Inside five minutes, I knew what I was doing right and what I was doing wrong as a parent, and no one had to tell me. It was as clear as day."

So a brilliant idea right? Well, I will say now that it was definitely gutsy. Not only did it take a very specific kind of family to agree to this procedure, but I frightened off 95 percent of the families we could have helped. Other professionals were stumped as to how to motivate their families to enroll in our process because most couldn't get over the hurdle of that scary video-camera stuff. It took years for professionals in our field to move past the guys-that-use-video-taping reputation, even though we realized the obstacle we had created and stopped using cameras within six months of implementing them.

Why would I tell you these awkward stories about our first families and our initial attempts to help them? It's simple, really: because you can't solve a difficult problem if you don't go "all in." At the time I started Homeward Bound, I remember reading studies that reported 50, 70, even 90 percent recidivism, depending on the issues being addressed. These dismal outcomes were not acceptable in my mind, as the best our field could produce. I was driven to find a solution to the problem of recidivism with the courage and gusto common to those who want to make a big difference. I suppose that the motivation I felt was similar in some respects, to what compelled others, such as Jim Bridger, to explore the West, or John Gottman to study marriage in the Love Lab.

We weren't savvy marketers; we were just determined to build a program and process that worked, regardless of whether it was hard or uncomfortable. The only criteria we used to determine if a certain feature should be included was the question, "Will this enhance the likelihood of success?" This level of commitment to a cause has led us on a great adventure of learning.

This book is meant to be life changing and for that to happen, both of us have to be willing to "go all in." I'm asking you to fully engage and buy into what I'm sharing, because if you do, your level of success will increase tremendously. Buying in means that you will use this book as a critical resource for self-development during the time your teen is in treatment and beyond. If you read it as intended, you will understand your role in your teen's current and past challenges and future success. You will become vulnerable and open to change, and I can't ask that of you without being equally open.

I hold in high esteem those first families (as well as the professionals who referred them to us) who taught us as much about how to help teens and families in transition as we taught them. Because we were blazing new trails, learning and developing our model as we went, I thought it only fair that I share with the first families the fact they were family number one, family number two, and family number three, and somehow, thankfully, they still opted to trust us. To maintain a good conscience and feel that we had given them good value for their money, I surprised each of them when we refunded a portion of their money. As I say, they were pleasantly surprised and a little confused by the refund, but they had given us a starting place to jump in and learn, which provided the foundation for the vast education we've received over the course of many subsequent years. So what were the foundational building blocks?

Three Major Factors for Long-Term Success

As I worked through the adolescent treatment outcome research following my experience with Garrett, I discovered there were themes that suggested best practices for increasing success after adolescent treatment. These themes were later identified in a review of the research by Heather Hair (2005), titled *Outcomes for Children and Adolescents after Residential Treatment: A Review of Research from 1993 to 2003*. Her objective was the same as mine, which was to "determine what factors increase the likelihood that positive individual and systemic changes occur for children and adolescents following discharge from residential treatment." After looking through a decade or more of outcome research, the bottom line was that the following three factors were key in predicting success levels long-term:

1. The extent to which the residents' families are involved in the treatment process before discharge;

2. The stability and structure of the place where the children or adolescents live after discharge;

3. The utilization of aftercare support for the children or youth and their families (Burns et al., 1999; Frensch and Cameron, 2002).

Interestingly, as Hair identifies, the importance of these factors has been noted in the residential treatment literature since the early 1970s (Charles and McIntyre, 1990; Ministry of Community and Social Services, 1978; Rae-Grant and Moffat, 1971; Taylor and Alpert, 1973) so at this point there is no question that these areas should be our focus.

Parent Involvement

Teens that have family, and particularly parents, involved in the treatment process, have better outcomes. Why is parental involvement so important? First, I'm sure that involvement for involvement's sake is not the key. Showing up at parent weekends simply to check the box will not give you the results you are looking for. The key is in the health of your family system. In one study I reviewed (Sunseri, 2004), treatment outcomes were highly associated with the level of family functioning, and involvement in the treatment program's processes helps increase a family's level of functioning. In addition, the same study showed that success was also associated with the teen "completing" the program. Parents who are engaged in the process are more likely to understand and buy into the approach being taken in treatment, and will therefore support treatment through to completion; and by so doing will improve the functioning of their family. The results of this study have significant implications for the treatment of children in residential care including the fact that treatment programs should be designed to do everything possible to support healthy development inside the family unit while the teen is in care.

During the process of treatment, most parents and their children experience some level of healing from the trauma that they had experienced prior to treatment. The issues prior to treatment are processed. Often both teens and their parents begin to take more individual responsibility for their part in the negative family dynamics, and with the support of the program, productive communication replaces the chronically conflictive interactions that had previously been the norm. Through better communication, the feelings family members have for one another will warm.

Involvement in the treatment of a child invites parents to look at themselves and seek to improve alongside their teen. Highly engaged parents tend to be open to learning and put themselves on a track of self-improvement.

There is only one corner of the universe you can be certain of improving, and that's your own self. —ALDOUS HUXLEY

As treatment provides a whole system for re-parenting teens, parents can watch how the professionals work with their son or daughter and glean principles and fresh approaches to their teen's issues. They can learn more about their teen's clinical challenges and often receive insights from the program's staff that can help later on after discharge. For example, when a young man diagnosed with oppositional defiant disorder (ODD) became agitated, his therapist was able to maintain a calm tone of voice, asking questions to help the youth process his feelings and talk himself down again. Parents witness for themselves the positive outcomes that result when the therapist does not take the outburst personally, is not emotionally triggered and has skills to help facilitate a good resolution of the problem.

Structure and Stability

Second, research suggests that the structure (the underlying design and pattern of a person's life consisting of daily routines, relationships with significant others, work, goals, etc.) and stability of the environment (emotionally and physically stable home life, clarity and consistency of expectations, etc.) that the teen is going home to are huge factors in long-term success. Why? Because environment has a powerful pull. This fact is precisely the reason you have taken your teen out of the home and placed that child in a specialized environment: to invite positive change. Turning your teen's life around without removing him or her from the old environment may be nigh unto impossible. Even in the best of homes, there is a big difference between the highly structured and safe milieu that teens experience in good programs, and the often inconsistent and haphazard approaches that result in most homes: far less structure, less support and frankly, a whole lot more complexity in relationships and life's challenges.

The environment is everything that isn't me. —**Albert Einstein**

Aftercare Process

Third, the involvement of the family, and particularly the parents, in the after-care process is vital. Out-of-home treatment is only the beginning. The real test, for both you and your teen, comes after discharge. While both of you have made personal changes, those changes will be put to the test in day-to-day living.

Your job will be to provide the stable leadership and the proper structure at home (or in the "real world") for the final transformational process to take place. Aftercare processes provide critical support to you and your teen as you endeavor to implement all that was learned while in treatment. With help to consistently apply the principles that I share in the chapters ahead, you will be able to establish new, healthy patterns signifying that you are well on your way to a successful transition and long-term success.

*A family is a place where principles are hammered and honed
on the anvil of everyday living.* —CHARLES R. SWINDOLL

Family System Focus

Did you notice that all three of the factors I cited from the research
have to do with the family? The importance of parental involvement
during treatment suggests the vital role of parenting for long-term
success. And sure enough, point number two—the importance of
a stable environment, providing the right structure and relationship
atmosphere for the returning teen—requires great input and leadership on the part of parents. Point number three—that the family
should be involved in the aftercare processes—further establishes
that this step is not easy, that it is not an individual teen endeavor
and that future success lies in creating a functional family capable of
dealing with the challenges each will face.

I recently spoke on the phone with a mother who said, "My
husband and I are seeing a marriage therapist right now because of
this whole thing with our son. The challenges he's put us through
have taken a huge toll on our marriage." Whether the teen's problems
are causing others in the family to develop issues, or vice versa, this
becomes a family system issue that must be resolved at the family
level for best results following treatment.

*In every conceivable manner, the family is link to our
past, bridge to our future.* —ALEX HALEY

In my work with individuals, families and larger human systems
such as in business organizations, I have become completely
convinced that you cannot understand individuals separately from

one another, and particularly, separately from their family. When you have an individual problem, there is always a larger system issue that needs to be addressed. To solve the problems of recidivism, treatment of the whole system is necessary. This calls for a family system approach. Very simply explained, this approach views individuals as interrelated and as having a significant influence on one another. A skilled clinician can discern the patterns of interaction that are repetitive and that cause a family or an individual to become stuck. Regard-less of the origin of the problem, the family system dynamics become patterned toward maintaining the status quo. When you're trying to produce a different outcome, the focus becomes one of breaking the cycles of interaction between family

> If it takes two to maintain a cycle, then it only takes one person to change it.

members and deliberately instituting new, healthier ways of interacting. I've always loved the truth that it takes two people to maintain a cycle because in its corollary there is great hope: if it takes two to maintain a cycle, then it only takes one person to change it.

So while our goal is to produce the systemic change that frees individuals to move forward and find better relationships and greater happiness, this is best accomplished as individuals within the family—focus on how they can do their part personally. Everyone has a role. To change yourself is to change the whole.

What If My Teen Is Not Coming Home?

If you are bringing your teen home after treatment, you probably understand how important it is to grow as a parent so that you can effectively reshape the relationship and the context of the home and family for when your teen comes home. But if your teen is 17 and nearing the magical age of 18, when he or she suddenly becomes an "adult," and is planning to live away from you, you might be asking, "Why do I need to worry about this? Isn't my adult child's launch into independent living the moment that I can finally relax? We all know I can't control things after that anyway."

Believe me, I understand the allure of that thinking. There is nothing you want more than to let go of the responsibility of continuing to manage your teen, especially after having had a break and feeling what it's like to be out from under that constant stress. But before you totally check out, let me give you five reasons why fully engaging in the family work of the program will still matter.

Five Reasons to Engage in Family Work

1. Keep in mind that you are still dealing with the same teen who needed to be placed in treatment a few months or years earlier. Many of these young adults will want independence, in a college setting or simply living apart from their family, but that doesn't mean they will be well equipped, right out of the program, to do so. It's likely that they will still require a great deal of parental involvement in spite of the fact they are living separately from the family home. Parents, you don't want to lose the gains you have sacrificed so much for.

2. Even those who are fairly well equipped need some time to ramp up. We know this because statistics show that even mature and responsible teens leaving home to live independently for the first time often crash and burn. First-year college students

too frequently drop out in their first semester for a myriad of reasons: They may be having difficulty balancing academic and social life. It might be that they can't get themselves up in the morning in time for classes, or they're struggling with loneliness, depression or anxiety. They might simply be partying too much. These are big challenges that can undo teens who have not required as much hand holding as your son or daughter probably has. The fact is that it's likely that your child will need you to stay involved in his or her life as a safety net (not a nest) on an ongoing basis for a while, post-treatment.

3. Many teens struggle with becoming self-motivated. This is often the case for teens with special needs as well. While you can't simply pour liquid motivation into them, you can help by creating the conditions in which they can find motivation and hang onto it. This requires a transition in your parenting style to give just the right degree of support while making them stand on their own two feet. Setting up the conditions for self-motivation requires parents to do some monitoring to ensure that the young adults are meeting their end of the bargain.

4. Managing the transition in your relationship from a dependent parent-child relationship to an independent adult-to-adult relationship is one of the most difficult things a parent will ever do, especially with a teen who has struggled as yours has. Finding the balance between letting go and giving the right amount of support is extremely challenging. It requires a lot

of emotional regulation and self-monitoring, skills that you can learn during your teen's time in treatment.

5. Young adults are rarely really "launched" these days and usually require several starts and stops before they are truly independent. The quality of your relationship, and unity with your co-parent, as your teen's independence fully emerges over the coming years, will facilitate the healthy launch that results in the kind of relationship that is neither dependent nor cut off but rather, interdependent.

I cover this transition more fully in Chapter 13. Basically, there is still work ahead and I'm here to help you finish strong. As you do, your results and your own peace of mind will be the payoff.

Molding the Context

You've undoubtedly heard the story of the frog thrown into a pot of boiling water. It immediately reacts by jumping out to save itself. But to boil that frog, you need only place it in room temperature water and slowly raise the heat until it boils. The frog doesn't notice what is happening until it is too late.

Our home environments are much the same. We may have let things slide and over time, things slowly fell out of order. We too may have slowly, imperceptibly drifted into a pattern of caretaking that fostered a sense of helplessness on the part of our teen, or we became tired and over time allowed more and more disrespectful behavior without consequences, or excessive gaming with few limits. If this entropy, or slide toward "chaos," is the case in your home, you are in good company. Every system on earth, if left to itself, dissolves into chaos.

Fortunately, as rational, thinking human beings, we have the ability and power to change our context and mold our environment. We can put energy into the system and remake our homes to produce healthier and happier family relationships and more stable emerging adults. But it does take energy—and a plan.

Have a Plan and Stick with It

Success depends upon previous preparation, and without such preparation there is sure to be failure. —CONFUCIOUS

One day I told a friend, "I hope I can make 2005 a better year." His immediate reply was, "Hope is not a strategy, Tim." It hit me humorously at first, because of his boldness and the way he just blurted it out, but then it rang true. He was right. Hope is a great place to begin because direction and action require it, but after that creative moment of reflection, we need a strategy or a plan in order to bring it about. Focus and consistent energy aimed at a desired goal doesn't come by chance.

In treatment, as in any lofty venture, having a well-thought-out plan in place and being able to follow the plan is what ultimately creates success. It isn't necessarily about the amount of money spent, or the

> It isn't necessarily about the amount of money spent, or the good intentions; it isn't even about the brilliance of the individuals involved. Planning, goal setting and preparation are key.

good intentions; it isn't even about the brilliance of the individuals involved. Planning, goal setting and preparation are key. You need knowledge and a plan to carry you through treatment and through the transitional challenges you will encounter afterward. Hope, along with the strategy, will inform your immediate steps when you read or hear the following, for example:

- Get me out of here! This is a horrible place you've sent me to. The kids here are so much worse than me.

- You never trust me or recognize the good things I'm doing. I'm going to just quit trying.

- You don't love me. I was sent away. You guys don't even want me around.

Your teen will do his or her best to dissuade you from your plan and make you feel that following through is not needed, or worse, that what you are doing (or did, if it's after treatment) is the wrong thing. You will also not always see eye to eye with the program, and teens, given that they are human too, will not always be perfect. The journey will have bumps. I want to help you understand that there is a tendency for some people, when the road becomes bumpy, to throw up their hands and look for someone to blame. Even parents who previously appreciated what was happening in treatment will sometimes find their commitment shaking, or their story shifting when their child starts to struggle.

As a neutral third party, let me warn you to beware of this trap. Second guessing usually only undermines and slows progress. Once you have made a good decision for treatment, it usually continues to be the right decision, even in difficult times. You did your homework. You asked family and friends for input. You used the best professional advice you could find before choosing a therapeutic milieu to foster growth in your son or daughter. Sticking with your decision and backing up the process is nearly always the best course to take.

That being said, on occasion, circumstances can change enough that it is necessary to reconsider. Your child may require a higher level of care, for example, or some other changing circumstance dictates that you look at alternatives. Consult with your professionals and then move forward again with confidence in what you decide. But remember, you don't need to remake the decision over and over again with each new crisis and with each challenge from your teen.

Teens May Have Agency, but Parents Have Empowerment

The teen years are challenging in any era. Can you remember how your social life suddenly became more complicated about the time you hit puberty? More was being demanded of you, academics got tougher, relationships became more dramatic, and your hormones started to fire, producing changes you weren't prepared for. You weren't shielded from the hard or scary things in life as you had been as a child. Then there was the peer pressure to do things that didn't sync with your parents' ideas of what was acceptable. As teens go through these changes, they are apt to withdraw or act out. If they don't have fields or forests to roam, they may spend too much time roaming the internet, or visiting their buddy's house, or exerting their energy and independence in a confrontational way. This naturally puts stress and pressure on the home and family. Even families that didn't have problems before adolescence, tend to have them now because the stress created finds all the weaknesses in a family system and brings them out big time.

The greatest weapon against stress is our ability to choose one thought over another. —William James

Crises in life, such as what happens as our adolescents are going through these changes, cry out for leadership. Our families need someone to lead the way out and up. They need clarity to replace the confusion, and someone to calm the system and draw each member back onto a positive growth track.

You have made a leadership decision to place your teen in the care of professionals. Now I am here to give you the understanding, the tools, and the level-headed empowerment necessary for you to continue the course you have started and ultimately, experience the most success possible. My task is to assist you in becoming the leader in your home that your unique teenager needs. This journey involves learning about how good treatment programs work and what your role is in maximizing their affect.

Summary
CHAPTER 1: ALL OR NOTHING: WHAT IT TAKES TO SUCCEED

- To get the most out of treatment, everyone, especially parents, has to commit to going "all in." Determine to engage sufficiently to understand your role in your teen's challenges as well as needed contributions to your teen's future successes.

- Research shows that the most significant factors for long-term success revolve around the family's level of involvement during treatment, the structure and stability of the home environment, and the participation of the family in aftercare services.

- Hope is not a strategy. Parents must have plans for how they will react to the bumps that inevitably come along the way during treatment and after the transition to home.

- Have a plan and stick with it. If you do your part and finish the treatment process, throughout the transition home, you'll have greater success and the entire family system can't help but change for the better.

CHAPTER 2

Know When to Hold 'Em: How Good Treatment Programs Work

"Tell me and I forget. Teach me and I remember. Involve me and I learn." —BENJAMIN FRANKLIN

As adults, we often feel we could do better if life offered us a reset button. We may not be abusing drugs or alcohol, but our lifestyle choices are affecting our relationships and mental health just the same.

Renee had turned heads since high school, and her long blond curls and engaging personality had made her a favorite with the young men at her university. The girls her age, though wary at first, were soon won over by her generous and empathetic nature. She was well loved.

She married a bit later in life, and not wanting to waste any time getting her family started, she had three children. Before she knew it, the varicose veins, graying hair, and ten years of sleep deprivation caught up with her. She was no longer able to place value or happiness on what she saw in the mirror, or what she accomplished in a day. What had worked to help her feel better so many times before, started to fail as she tried to bolster her sagging spirits through service to others, such as taking dinner to an elderly grandparent or watching a neighbor's child so the parent could steal an afternoon away. Nothing she tried (e.g., a new dress, a completed home project, exercise, etc.) seemed to help. With each child, the exhaustion compounded, the baby weight multiplied, and she sunk further into the darkness of depression. She was no longer the vivacious and healthy person she had once been.

Finally, in a crisis, her family members urged her to go online and look for help. While this problem was not hers alone, there were definite issues within her family that caused stress, she wasn't about to walk away from her children and husband. She loved them and they loved her. At the same time, she couldn't give up serving others, because it was in her nature to do so. But it had finally become self evident that she couldn't continue living as she was, or she would end up suffering a nervous breakdown.

Finding a health spa, she gulped at the price but, encouraged by her family, she enrolled in a three-week program. With the help of neighbors and family to watch the home front, Renee checked in, was assigned to her room and given specific instructions as to what was expected, what was available to her, what was allowed and what translated into the greatest success for weight loss and healing in the three-week program.

Anxious but excited, she resolved to be the best resident that spa had ever worked with. She got up early, drank her water, went on every hike available, took cooking classes, prayed, attended Zumba and yoga classes, read, journaled and took time for meditation.

At the end of her three weeks, she had lost 23 pounds, but what was most exceptional to her loved ones and herself was the rebirth of the old Renee. She was glowing, centered and secure. Gone were the fragmented conversations and frantic overscheduling of her days. She tapped back into the powerful person she was, learned how to cope with her most triggering stressors and was committed to maintaining her healthy new lifestyle.

Elements of a Powerful Therapeutic Milieu

You might be thinking that if you scored three weeks at a health spa, you'd get healthy too. Why is that? It's because we all know instinctively that the environment that surrounds us has a massive affect on us. In the case of Renee, she experienced the transformative influence of a *thera-*

> Each aspect of the physical, social and emotional environment is consciously designed to be "therapeutic" for its residents.

peutic milieu. After life became intolerable, she deliberately placed herself in an environment where each aspect of the physical, social and emotional environment is consciously designed to be "therapeutic" for its residents.

You are considering placing your teen into such an environment—or perhaps you have already done so. In the pages ahead I want to describe some of the common elements of a good therapeutic environment so you can fully support and participate in the creation of an experience suited specifically for your teen.

A therapeutic program is specifically set up to stop the downward spiral of a teen's behavior and change the trajectory to an upward one. When a teen is removed from the stressors and triggers of home, with life slowed down to a manageable pace, and then placed in an environment with staff, activities and therapy designed to encourage change, the opportunity for the kind of true and deep change required to turn that teen's life around may never be greater. After making what many parents say was "the hardest decision of my life," you can begin to feel hope again, thinking of what an opportunity this treatment experience presents for your teen and for your family at large.

Distance not only gives nostalgia, but perspective and maybe objectivity. —ROBERT MORGAN

Many of these teens are behind their peers in terms of emotional maturity, academics and personal coping skills and in many cases have become self-destructive to the point where their parents feel that they are left with very few choices. Most kids mature and grow over time, but in cases in which teens are in crisis, they can do permanent damage to their life opportunities if an intervention is not made. Putting your son or daughter into a therapeutic milieu that's specifically designed to meet their challenges can help them mature emotionally by a factor of two years in their development in

> Take the time as you read through this section to learn how therapeutic programs work. Take note of the principles used in programs that you can apply in your home.

perhaps just nine months, according to some treatment professionals I interviewed for this book. Good programs purposefully design powerful milieus that tend to include similar foundational characteristics and elements. Take the time as you read through this section to learn how therapeutic programs work. Take note of the principles used in programs that you can apply in your home.

A well-crafted therapeutic milieu supercharges the environment to enhance the likelihood and speed of change. The foundation of such an environment is the creation of a safe, relationally warm place where a young person is protected from self-destructive behavior, unburdened from the "overwhelm" of life, and immersed in a relational climate that invites introspection. Such a place enables young people to look at their choices, their personal limitations, and the outcomes of the strategies they are using, and to recognize their own contributions to their problems and unhappiness. From a basic, high-level vantage point, effective treatment programs share common elements:

- A full and balanced daily life structure and schedule;

- Clinical support through individual and group therapy;

- Constant exposure to positive role models and coaching from staff;

- A positive peer culture in which teens who have progressed influence other teens in positive ways;

- Clear and consistent expectations and rules;

- Experiential and recreational activities;

- Methods for defining and recognizing progress;

- Academic programming and support;

- Parent education and involvement in the treatment process.

Now let me go into a few of these elements more completely.

Consistency Is King

While every program has its own unique therapeutic culture, an effective therapeutic milieu maintains consistency in its "parenting" philosophy, structure, expectations and purpose. But staff are not just instituting structure and imposing boundaries on the teens. Staff members are role models of the program's philosophy. When the program is done well staff demonstrate in word, deed and through repeated example how to "be."

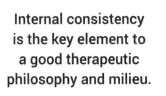

Internal consistency is the key element to a good therapeutic philosophy and milieu.

With all of the variety in therapeutic programs, internal consistency is the key element to a good therapeutic philosophy and milieu. It's within a consistent and predictable setting that group members can anticipate the results of their choices and find the safety to work through their emotional, psychological and social issues most effectively.

Ideally, all the members of a program, from the top down to the frontline staff, understand what they are trying to accomplish with their clients, and exactly how that is supposed to occur. Regular staff trainings are internal processes aimed at achieving this shared vision. Tony Mosier, a cofounder of a residential treatment center for boys, advises visiting parents to ask the frontline staff, "What is it about your program that changes lives? How does that process occur?" If that staff member can talk for 15 minutes about the process in detail, and about the values and components involved, that's probably a good program.

Such an interview would suggest that everyone on the team understands the plan, and where that is the case, there is more likely to be consistency among the staff in applying the principles of that plan. I'm sure you can imagine how important this is; you may even have first-hand experience of how lack of consistency between caregivers impacts the family—for example, concerning chores, curfews, behavior, and so on. Even small issues can become almost impossible to manage or work though when there is a wide gap between each parent's philosophies. Progress can't be made. It's confusing and chaotic, and ultimately, teens don't thrive in such a situation. So it goes in programs as well. In good programs there exists a consistency of philosophy and practice that everybody can count on. In fact, I would take it one step further to say that in good programs the staff actually come to have an allegiance to the program's model. There is evidence that "allegiance" is a more powerful predictor of therapeutic success than the model itself. Wamphold (2001) contends that when therapists have a strong allegiance to a treatment model, they will practice the treatment with a higher level of skill, enthusiasm, hope and tenacity, all of which would certainly supercharge the treatment effect.

Success is neither magical nor mysterious. Success is the natural consequence of consistently applying basic fundamentals. —JIM ROHN

Safety and Security

Mary Alexine, co-founder of a girls' residential program in Montana, said that her hope "is to give students a chance to really have time out from the pressures of the world and be immersed in a setting that is monitored and controlled, an environment that's both protective and stimulating, serving up rich experiences, good relationships, good values, and solid principles."

A controlled, consistent environment replaces the toxic environment they're leaving. They don't have access to drugs or alcohol. The influence of their buddies is cut off. If they've been struggling academically, often there are underlying special needs that are addressed in this new and unique academic environment. If there was contention at home, the destructive cycles with siblings and parents are stopped and communication is deliberately slowed down to include exchanges through letters, mediated conversations, and intermittent visits. This completely changes the dynamic and stops parents and teens from engaging in the same ineffective communication patterns used before. It's as if the pause button is pushed and teens eventually are able to move away from their rigid perspectives and look at their relationships from a new and clear vantage point. They begin to gain perspective on the life events that perhaps created trauma, or on their contribution to the "mess" their lives have become. They learn about their own unique emotional and cognitive make up and their problems or limitations as a starting point for the journey forward.

Once we accept our limits, we go beyond them. —ALBERT EINSTEIN

When we talk about safety in a treatment program, most parents think first about physical safety, because they've probably seen their teens so out of control that their safety has been jeopardized—for example, temper tantrums, cutting, running away, sexual promiscuity, drug abuse, violence and other highly impulsive actions. But I want to expand the definition of safety to help you understand that a good therapeutic environment needs to not only protect teens physically but also engender a feeling of emotional safety. When teens who are at high risk of harming themselves first enter a program, out of necessity the primary focus must be on keeping them physically safe. As they progress beyond being considered a risk, they can recognize the emotional safety created by the milieu, which is an essential element in a teen's development. Good programs hold a teen securely but lovingly, thus creating a sense of safety in both senses of the word. Teens in such settings not only feel protected from their own self-destructive tendencies but they also have a chance to feel loved by others outside their normal caregivers.

Think back to the time you held a new baby. Perhaps you remember when your teen was still just a bundle of joy in a blanket. How did you hold that baby to calm and comfort her when she was distressed? You probably checked the clock to make sure the baby had been fed recently, that there wasn't a dirty diaper or a rash making the her uncomfortable, and you determined if she was warm or cool enough. If that all looked good, you probably picked her up, held her securely in a blanket, careful not to squeeze her too hard but kept her arms from flailing, and spoke soothing words as you walked or rocked until she calmed down. Time in a good therapeutic program does the same thing for a teen—minus the swaddling.

I remember a young man with whom I worked in the wilderness and who came to us with significant paranoia. Early in his stay with us he was highly anxious almost all the time. Anytime he was with me in a therapy session, he constantly looked around to make sure no one was sneaking up on him. His paranoia led him to believe that the planes flying overhead were actually government spies, or law enforcement looking for him. This was especially hard on him, given that our field was close to a military base and we saw dozens of airplanes every day. Within a few weeks in the wilderness milieu, surrounded by staff who cared for him and held him accountable, his paranoia disappeared. He stopped worrying about the planes and about everything else that had consumed his thoughts. His mother commented to me that she had never seen him trust anyone before being with us and that he was as content and at peace "in the wild" as she had ever seen him. The milieu, not me as his therapist alone, produced a sense of security he had never before attained.

A Structured Full Daily Schedule

A significant part of the therapeutic milieu is how the time in a program is spent and the activities students engage in. Programs tend to feel that there isn't enough time in the day to fit in all the good things they would like their students to experience. They also know that teens who have too much time on their hands, unless they are out in nature without electronics, tend to get in trouble or not use it in productive ways. Their goal is to provide growth opportunities to the students through a variety of activities ranging from physical fitness, education, wholesome recreational activities, service opportunities, individual and group therapy, and work projects. While they do have times when they can reflect and pause, in most cases, daily life in a program is full and has a consistency to it. Students retire to bed and get up at the appointed time. There is a time set for each meal of the day. Students can count on it.

Students thrive under these conditions. Consistency provides a sense of security from which they can learn to take on the challenges that come into their life. Change is difficult for many people, let alone most teens, who would much prefer change within a framework of consistency that they can count on. Structure also helps them develop discipline. Before they can eat, for example, their room needs to be clean and their beds made. In some cases these disciplines have been severely undermined at home as the teen began to refuse to follow routines or abide by the requests of their parents' but in structured therapeutic settings, these disciplines can be learned and the teen's confidence tends to grow as a result.

Clinical Component

Although a good therapeutic milieu is made up of far more than the individual therapist, these professionals do play a significant role in treatment. Program culture is significantly influenced by the therapists as many treatment programs are managed by clinical professionals, and all of them rely heavily on their expertise. Finding the right therapist for a given client population is important as not every therapist can be exceptional in all areas. But where a program specializes in a certain clinical population, members of the clinical staff generally have honed their experience working with those types of issues and as such, are great resources for you to tap into. In addition to their expertise, these are professionals who like teens and have a good relationship-based approach with them. Experts use their knowledge as well as the warmth, the respect, the trust and the experience they possess to inspire the teen, and at times confront the teen to make changes in their attitude toward the world. Teens benefit from individual one-on-one therapy as well as group therapy. And although the therapeutic milieu is prepared to reduce stressors and temptations, there are ample opportunities on a daily basis for teens to learn from the expert guides around them.

Paula Leslie, a therapist and educational consultant by profession, shared with me one of the great plusses to a good therapeutic program in these words: "In programs, there's a lot of tag-teaming happening. So if a particular behavior for the young person is really wearing, whereas a parent may give in or alter an expectation just because they're worn down, a good therapist (or staff member) can maintain a calm, consistent response and expectation for weeks, or months, or for however long it takes for the young person to be able to respond in an effective way."

Good Staff

In addition to trained clinical professionals, in my opinion, the most powerful—and often overlooked—factor is good staff, because a program is only as good as the frontline people who interact with the teens every day, all day. High-quality therapeutic programs seek out excellent staff, people who are in the field because they care about and really want to help teenagers. Many can deeply connect with the kind of kids that are in that program. So, even outside therapy, there's opportunity on a moment-to-moment basis for teens to be mentored, coached and even corrected when need be. They're continually observing and interacting with positive role models who often aren't much older than themselves. In high-quality therapeutic programs, staff-student relationships tend to be less hierarchical and more often have an element of friendship.

Another educational consultant, Jenny Heckman, told me, "In good treatment programs there are elements of both objectivity and caring. Inside families, things can be much more emotional. In a treatment program, I see staff who really care about the kids but are less emotionally locked into (or triggered by) the children or young people as a parent tends to be."

Deeper, more personal relationships tend to develop between staff and students, and can be the strongest invitation to teens to change and improve themselves. They are available when a student is ready to talk because they are there with the teens 24/7: at the campfire as they whittle a flute, on the hike when they form blisters and want to quit, in the arena when they get dumped by a horse or in the computer lab when the frustration mounts. Staff members are ever-present, while therapists often have to be told what happened the day before. All parents should pray that their sons or daughters develop a deep connection to at least one staff member in their program.

Lucy Pritzker, an educational consultant with a special-needs son of her own says, "Programs can provide the structure some kids need, where home life can be chaotic. When I would tell the family that dinner would be ready at six o'clock, sometimes it would be, and sometimes it wouldn't. The phone might ring, the dog might need to be let out, or there could be a soccer practice that goes over time. In a treatment program they have numerous staff to make sure dinner is on the table at six. That kind of structure is so important to some kids."

When I was at Outback, I got to see some incredibly gifted staff working with students. I sometimes felt that I was cheating, frankly, as a therapist. I would go out to the field once or twice a week and do my sessions, and believed I was making a real difference. But the progress I saw between sessions was far greater. Mother nature and our staff were the real heroes. I always felt a little uncomfort-able—and would quickly spread the credit around—when parents thanked me for the progress they were seeing in their child. Dr. Bryan Zitzman, our program director, often asks teens who return home, "Who would you say influenced you the most during your time at the program?" He says that about 80 percent of the time they give him a name other than that of their therapist. When he asks who these influencers are, the teens mention staff ranging all the way from field staff to the chef. It is the same at home in the real world. It's rarely a therapist who makes the most difference, which is just one reason why it is so important to build a natural support system of neighbors, friends and family when the teen returns home; but more about that later. Good treatment programs have good staff, because they're a vital aspect of the milieu they're fostering.

Parent Participation

Good programs are always looking to improve the effectiveness of their treatment and over the years the field as a whole has tapped into many ideas that have done just that. But the greatest way to move the needle is still mostly untapped. I know of nothing that gives treatment a quantum leap in success like when parents are enlisted in the process on day one, and then supported in the right way after treatment. Engaging parents during treatment is critical, continued after treatment... game changing!

> Engaging parents during treatment is critical; continued after treatment... game changing!

Parents are enlisted on two fronts. First, as an expert on their child to offer insights and guidance for the treatment team throughout the journey. No one knows or loves your child like you do. And second, which is the crux of this book, parents are engaged in a journey of personal and family development to prepare themselves for their teens' return.

Family therapy on a regular basis will enable you to hone your skills, gather insight into your teen, and provide a forum for you to communicate with your son or daughter to build your relationship on solid ground again. Eventually the time will come for your adolescent to come home for a visit and "practice" being together again in the natural home environment. This is a wonderful therapeutic tool that is employed in programs as a small test of your teen's new skills. Let me share the purpose and vision for these home visits so you can make the most of them.

Parents who hope for a "perfect" home visit are usually disappointed. Expect that there will be mistakes made during these visits. Mistakes, in fact, provide the fodder for big surges in treatment once teens return to the program. Both weaknesses and strengths are exposed, giving the therapist more information to work with going forward.

Dan Stuart, a gifted clinician and cofounder of a girls' residential program, says, "Home visits are considered therapeutic interventions! Many of our students think of family visits as a break from treatment, but we consider them to be some of the most therapeutic opportunities we have. We are, after all, working to improve the relationship between parent and daughter and preparing her to return home to live with the family. These visits provide us with our best data as to how she is progressing toward that end. Because of this, home visits are carefully planned and include specific therapeutic goals and structure to provide for the best possible experience. We encourage parents to look forward to these visits as interventions and not vacations."

He continues, "The other factor that parents should prepare for is that home visits do not always go as hoped. Teens often make mistakes at home or demonstrate some type of regression, poor judgment or give in to temptation. Sometimes these mistakes are minor and sometimes they can be major. The important thing to remember is that mistakes are inevitable and are an important part of the therapeutic process. Since home visits are "tests" of a young person's development, they do not always "pass." In fact, the mistakes they make teach us a great deal about what "weak spots" may still exist and what areas are in need of continued refinement. To this end, we actually count on mistakes being made. This provides parents and the treatment team with a wealth of information regarding continued therapeutic needs. We ready our students to help them recognize their mistakes and setbacks as "feedback" instead of "failures."

> Mistakes are inevitable and are an important part of the therapeutic process.

> *It's fine to celebrate 2 but it is more important to heed the lessons of failure.* —BILL GATES

Let me make two additional points about home visits. First, visits should not result in you putting life "on hold" so you can spend all your time with your teen. This too is part of the test of how well your son or daughter is progressing toward being ready to return home. Second, it is not a time to indulge your teen with food, gifts or the power to choose or veto every decision. Siblings will often resent this if it occurs, and you will imply that you feel bad your teen is in the program and you are likely to try and "make it up" to him or her.

This behavior encourages teens to complain more about the program and all the things they are missing out on at home. Simply put, they sense your guilt and play on it.

Individualized Treatment

There is a buzzword used in the treatment world—individualized treatment—that I need to explain. This is a powerful concept that parents can learn from. What "individualized treatment" means is that the program can meet teens where they are and build from there. In other words, the approach is not a one-size-fits-all kind of rigid structure. The program is not scripted out. While programs accept a particular type of teenager, within that category of challenges they have a plan and a model for encouraging change. Within certain limits they are able to individualize and meet teenagers wherever they happen to be.

Each young person is a unique individual who possesses his or her own set of strengths, weaknesses and personal style. Progress is enhanced as the milieu delivers up conversations, experiences, consequences and interventions customized to them. Though the program starts with a general treatment plan, it is invariably altered and customized as the treatment team gains intimate knowledge of that particular student.

Let me illustrate with an example. I worked with a young woman who had completed a wilderness program and was home again. One of the keys to success in her case was her parents' reestablishment of the leadership hierarchy in their home. As predicted, she resisted this change—because what teen happily gives up control? I was fortunate enough to live close to her family. On my way to our farm one day, I stopped by with the horses and took Millie, her mother and father all riding. Millie happened to love horses and in that brief hour, she opened up, drawing her own parallels with how her behavior could be compared to a wild horse, and how her parents' attempts to control her were needed and helpful in keeping her safe, productive and happy. I can't take all our students riding—and riding isn't inherently magical—but I can flex our model in some ways to meet them where they are. Good treatment programs, and especially good parenting, do the same.

While individualizing treatment is an important principle, it is also important to understand that it is the program's call on which aspects are appropriate to bend, and which ones should remain solid. You may suggest an idea, but it's not helpful when you become demanding of flexibility or exceptions. Such decisions are more complex than they appear, with the potential for unintended consequences not just for your teen but also for the others in the program. Individualizing treatment essentially means tailoring the program's climate, culture and some aspects of the model to meet the needs of that particular teenager and to see the most rapid progress physically, psychologically, emotionally, developmentally, relationally, socially and culturally.

Jared Balmer, founder of a number of residential programs and a man I greatly respect, puts it this way, "Individualized treatment interventions are tailored to the individual client/student and are not unilaterally applied across a given population. Based on this definition, all programs are faced with the burden to determine what (within their program) *is* individualized and what *is not*."

Time

There is another element to why good programs work and that is simply time. There's a common metaphor in our industry for the process of treatment. It is likened to baking bread in terms of the importance of keeping bread in the oven long enough to bake all the way through. Bringing the bread out of the oven prematurely can significantly affect the form and "doneness" of the loaf. To create deep, internal change, teens need to be immersed in a carefully crafted milieu, with positive values and solid principles, long enough for these changes to sink in.

If you don't have time to do it right, when will you have time to do it over? —JOHN WOODEN

Another wonderful metaphor is given by Dr. John McKinnon, cofounder of a coed therapeutic boarding school. He describes adolescence as a period when we metaphorically need to pick up speed to merge onto the freeway of life. Adulthood requires that we are able to go at a good clip in order to thrive in society. Some students, for reasons such as processing issues, trauma, depression or other issues, find that their "driving skills" aren't sufficient to reach the needed speeds to merge into society without causing disruption to those around them and to themselves. They are not keeping pace or driving safely and are creating havoc in life for themselves and others. Time in a therapeutic treatment program allows them to get off the freeway, diagnose and repair what's not working and then ramp their speed up to where they can safely merge back into the flow of teenage life again, this time, hopefully, with all the gears needed to move with the flow of traffic.

Listen as best as you can to the recommendations of your treatment program staff for when your teen is ready to "merge" back into life. They know their milieu. They understand what it takes to help teens make these breakthroughs and start to internalize the necessary skills, attitudes and self-understanding, and they have a sense of timing for when they are ready. In most cases therapeutic programs include a level system: teens can progress in different areas and their growth is acknowledged by moving them up a level. Sometimes teens regress and this is addressed by moving them down a level. Each level is associated with progressive freedoms, privileges and responsibilities. This "concrete" approach is designed to help teens understand more clearly the connection between their actions and consequences. The choice-consequence linkage is made overt as the program processes, corrects and celebrates the choices that teens make. In this process teens are minutely examining the impact their actions are having on their lives. This provides immediate motivation for either a direction change, or continuance in behavior. Can you imagine if your actions were given that kind of thoughtful attention each day? You couldn't be kept from improving yourself dramatically.

While some programs do not employ a level system—because there is some debate as to whether there are populations that don't respond well to level systems as a means of acknowledging growth or regression—all effective programs have ways to teach values, expand a teen's insight and make the outcomes of good or poor choices more obvious to the child or teen.

Therapeutic programs generally have a flexible length of stay—not a set amount of time or a semester enrollment—based on how the teen is progressing. You may be saying to yourself, "Yes, of course. Every teen is unique and his or her journey or timing is going to be unique as well." But let me forewarn you that staying committed to a flexible length of stay can be hard even though doing so makes perfect sense right now. Money gets tight. Special occasions you don't want your son or daughter to miss come along, and the temptation to pull your teen out a bit early is compelling. Parents, please allow the program to guide you in understanding how long your teen needs to stay. If I can give you a warning—because I can guarantee this will come up—do not allow the calendar to do the decision making. For example, "Christmas is coming and we'd really like her to be home for that; everyone will be in town and they all want to see her. Let's have that be the timeline for her to be finished." Back to the baking analogy: you don't want to stop the process before it's complete, because the results won't be as good or have the staying power they would have if you'd given the program enough time to achieve the desired results.

Amelia

Amelia was in a well-respected residential treatment program, but her parents, who were being helped with the finances by an outside agency, were unsure how long that help would be available to them. Though both Mom and Dad were working professionals, an extra $6,000 per month was not something they could come up with. They informed the program that this would need to be a month-to-month situation. As a result, they were constantly anticipating a transition home, thus hampering the therapeutic process. The therapist and staff were reluctant to move ahead in addressing Amelia's deeper issues because of the risk of leaving things open, ugly, and unresolved right when she would need strength and confidence for the transition. Knowing that she might be pulled out at any time, they had to focus solely on the surface issues to help Amelia see at least *some* progress. One of the most powerful ways you can encourage your teen to give his or her best effort is to send the message that you are in full support of taking whatever amount of time it requires for him or her to reach the therapeutic goals that have been set. This level of commitment on your part, paradoxically, has the power to speed up the process.

> Send the message that you are in full support of taking whatever amount of time it requires for him or her to reach the therapeutic goals that have been set.

When I first met Amelia in her treatment program as her family's transition coach, I could tell that this girl had her bags packed and waiting; actually, they'd never been unpacked. She was just biding her time before the money ran out and she was free to get back to living her life. I was introduced to her treatment team during their clinical meeting. It was incredibly helpful to listen to their assessments, the treatment plan and the concerns. I was able to weigh in on the process because I was working with the family on the home front in tandem with the program's work with Amelia, so I was able to advocate for more time with the agency. Once the program staff knew they had four more months to work with her, they were able to open things up in therapy, and confront her more aggressively on her destructive thinking, knowing that she had time to digest everything and assimilate new strategies before going home. A whopping 90 percent of the progress she made in treatment was accomplished in that four-month block, compared to only about 10 percent in the six months prior.

Summary
CHAPTER 2: KNOW WHEN TO HOLD 'EM:
HOW GOOD TREATMENT PROGRAMS WORK

- A therapeutic milieu is a carefully crafted experience and setting meant to address a particular population's mental, social, emotional, physical and relational growth needs.

- Individualized treatment and a flexible length of stay means that a program can be customized to meet the needs of individual teens. Some aspects of a program can be flexed and some cannot, but the goal is to meet each teen where they are.

- Consistency is king. All programs have a philosophy of change and consistency is key to that goal of change. Clinical professionals and frontline staff strive to create a predictable and safe environment for a teen to trust, work and grow in.

- Home visits are a critical piece of the treatment, affording the program staff, the teen and the family important data for what "weak spots" may still exist and need continued refinement.

What to Do Now

I'm sure as you began your family, you considered—whether formally or not—the type of the home you wanted to create. Take some time now to consider which aspects of the "milieu" you envisioned then, have been successfully implemented. What aspects are missing and what do you want to do about it?

CHAPTER 3

Ready to Roll: Your Role While Your Teen is in Treatment

"INTENT reveals desire; ACTION reveals commitment." —STEVE MARABOLI

efore you read this chapter's title and teeter on the brink of being overwhelmed, let me tell you a quick story. We have a dear friend, Heather, who was a cheerleader in college. Twenty years and five children later, she still bubbles and enthuses and encourages everyone in whatever they are attempting. Heather came over to see what my wife had done with a shed that she had recently organized to hold our camping and emergency supplies, because she wanted to do something similar. Heather stood there with her arms at her side just staring for a moment. Then she turned with a smile and said "I can be overwhelmed … or motivated. I choose motivated!"

This is the response I expect from an engaged parent as well. I understand how intimidating the task before you looks. But I also know that you can eat an elephant … one bite at a time. *Writing* this book felt like eating an elephant. If you can be motivated to take just 20 percent of the advice held herein and determine that, if nothing else, you will do (blank), that's a great start. Now if that 20 percent happens to contain the principles most critical to your success, you have just tapped into the 80/20 rule, the Pareto principle, or the law of the vital few. It is a common law in business, for example, that 80 percent of your profits come from 20 percent of your customers, and 80 percent of your profits come from 20 percent of the time you spend, and so on. If you pick the right 20 percent, you will have 80 percent of the results you seek.

I'm going to be completely transparent with you: my goal for this chapter is to pull you all the way in and help you fully engage in the treatment process from the start. As we've seen, family involvement during the treatment process is one of the big keys to long-term success. So, with an eye toward that goal, let's get to work!

Before I launch into what you can do as parents to improve your future success, let me acknowledge something that is not said nearly often enough: I know you have a very tough job as a parent. I often share stories or blog about the challenges of raising my own kids, because they are humbling, even in the best of cases. In the more difficult cases, many of you have a child who has tested your limits from birth, or who has grappled with severe issues as he or she moved into adolescence. As I've come to intimately know the family makeup and trials faced by so many in your shoes, I long ago stopped passing judgment on parents' failure to rein things in, or let go or stay calm. More often than not, I have been amazed at the endurance of parents in dealing with their struggling teen. For some, the investment financially and emotionally has been 100 percent and then some. So, if you ever feel like a failure as a parent, or sense that others judge your parenting skills harshly because you have a teen who is struggling, just know that there are those of us who understand. As for the rest, they have their own problems in other arenas of life and probably don't view you nearly as critically as you imagine. Most parents who have a struggling teen feel this way. It's human nature to think that if things are not going well in a particular area, that must mean that we're pathetic at it. Beating ourselves up just comes naturally to some of us. I love how Bryan Zitzman explains this to parents in the following metaphor:

> Have you ever seen another parent struggling with a parenting situation in a public place? You might have even caught yourself thinking of what they should do differently. But then again, given that you're reading this book, chances are you have one or more children who haven't been the easiest children to raise. So it's highly likely that you would refrain from passing judgment in those situations, which is exactly what we all should do.

> The truth is some children are simply easier to raise than others. Raising those children is like hitting a five-foot bull's eye from a distance of 20 feet away. And most parents, even without a parenting manual, can be involved enough, loving enough, patient enough, consistent enough—you name it—that those children will "turn out" just fine. They'll keep most of the rules most of the time. They'll accept "no" without too much push back. They'll do well in school and require moderate nudging and effort to keep them moving in the right direction. In

general, the basics of good parenting will be sufficient and we'll feel good about our parenting.

However, not all children are quite so easy. Some have difficult temperaments. Others have mental health issues. Still others may have experienced trauma of some kind. The list goes on, but the bottom line is this: parenting those children is like hitting a one-foot bull's eye from a distance of 20 feet away! And if you take a parent who is used to shooting at that "five-foot bull's eye" and you put that parent across from a "one-foot bull's eye," let's just say they tend to develop a little empathy.

This doesn't mean we accept that they are difficult children to raise and leave it at that. It means that as parents raising these children, we want to learn, practice, and refine our skills until we become good at hitting that one-foot bull's eye. That may mean getting really good at staying calm. It may mean being more consistent in how we handle situations, or clearer in our communication than the average parent. It may be about learning to pick our battles wisely. It may mean becoming really good at speaking our child's language. Whatever it might be, we do what it takes because we love them just as much and we know it's what they need from us as their parents.

So, the next time you see another parent struggling with a child in a public place, not only will you feel the empathy you've always felt for them, but you'll likely think to yourself, "There's a one-foot bull's eye situation. I know what that's like."

It's Your Turn

Now that your son or daughter is in treatment and making changes thanks to the new context he or she is in, it's time for you to consider the context at home and see what needs to change there as well.

Why? Picture the family system as a puzzle with all the different pieces being the individuals in your family, the environment, friends, technology, and so on, and your teen being the puzzle piece at the center. Imagine that you take him or her out of the middle of that puzzle (the home/family context) and mold, change and reshape that piece, through the therapeutic process of treatment. When it is returned to the puzzle, if the pieces surrounding that reshaped piece are rigidly holding to the same shape as before, those surrounding pieces will cause the malleable one to eventually return to its former shape to fit in. The *hole* needs to be adapted to fit the newly shaped piece; the surrounding pieces are the ones that need to become malleable, to create a space that invites the returning piece to retain its new and improved shape.

For me, a lot of the difficulty of change was based on my self-image as a parent. I had to give up on this idea that my parenting was sort of perfect. I had to be a little more humble about it and yet take it on in a different way. I don't know if all parents who have gone through a program have those insights—maybe

they will get it from reading this book—but you really need
to get off your high horse. —PARENT (CALIFORNIA)

Turning your child over to relative strangers when they are so fragile or troubled most likely went against every instinct you have as a parent. You hand your child over to someone, everyone is crying, and then you walk out the door. The sense of guilt, shame and most likely confusion over what to do may have kept you from making the decision until things had escalated to a point where you could no longer handle the situation. Please understand that you are not alone in your crisis or in your thinking.

I just remember something I had to sign at the program that had
to do with state regulations. Basically it was the last thing asked
of me to sign and it explained something along the lines that we
were certifying that we were leaving our child in Utah, from DC,
and that basically the program was going to take the place of the
parent. I was not thrilled with my co-parent, but I remember going
back to the hotel we were staying in and I just looked at him. We
sat down and had something to eat together and I just said, "This
is the weirdest thing we have ever done." And it really didn't feel
too good. It was a relief, but we felt like we had to admit that we
had failed to take care of this kid and parent her in the way she
needed. It was very humbling. —PARENT (WASHINGTON, DC)

The Résumé of Failure

Tim Clark, author of *Employee Engagement Mindset*, suggests to the executives that he coaches that, as a complement to their regular résumé, which lists out their achievements, they also create a résumé of their failures, because those failures are equally as responsible for the person's experience, character and strengths as the successes are. Before we go any farther on our journey, I'd like you to take an hour to create your own. It's a simple exercise but definitely not easy.

I want you to do this exercise for two reasons: first, so it becomes more obvious to you how you developed the strengths you have as a result of living through and processing some of your failures—the same reason Tim Clark encourages his clients to do so. Second, this exercise will help you to make the frank personal assessment you need in order to know where to start working on yourself. I do realize that I've just finished telling you to give yourself a break, or at least a little compassion, because you have a challenging teen, and that most of us would struggle as much or more than you if we were in your shoes. All that is still true. But I know you can do more and achieve more happiness and success with your teen as a result. Writing a personal résumé of failure will get you to do one tough task that if shunned or avoided, will shrink, if not doom, your family system's potential. The critical point is to vividly see how *you*—not your spouse or ex-spouse, not your teen, or some other person—are feeding and propagating the problem. Once these weaknesses have been identified by you, the power to change blossoms.

Why inflict this kind of pain on ourselves? Because we all fail, but the tragedy is in not learning from our failures. This list is something to be proud of, because you are going to learn from these experiences. You are going to plumb the depths to look for the triggers, for the meaning and for the strengths that were born from these depths. If you take this exercise seriously, you will thank me for it later. Just as your teen's issues and your family situation are unique, there exist strengths and resources that are unique to you as well. Life is not a big gamble. You can control *yourself*, even if you can't control your

Résumé of Failure

This exercise is for your personal benefit. If you would like to review or share it with others, you may want to write your list and explanations down. If you know yourself well, and that you tend to get bogged down with writing assignments, feel free to talk to a mirror, or imagine reviewing your résumé with me over your kitchen table.

Step 1: Number a sheet of paper 1 through 10. Now, list ten (not two or three) personal, family and parenting failures, the spectacular fiascoes. You don't need to categorize them; just get them down—any addictions, conflict, abuse, losses, profes-sional decisions or disappointments that have contributed to your relationship challenges. Failures are some of the most formative and defining experiences of our lives, and we want to look at what makes you *you.*

Step 2: Explain what happened and why. Keep it brief, but give a little context for each failure.

Step 3: Write down or tell me what you learned and felt from each failure. Be brutally honest and don't pull any punches.

Step 4 (my addition to the exercise): Based on this experience, identify one thing about yourself that you will change. You may now be aware of something you did that you need to stop doing, or something you didn't do enough of that you need to start doing. Whatever seems to be most critical in producing a healthy family system for your teen to return to, write it down. Commit to changing this one, most imperative weakness into a strength. You have time and space now to do so. If you are really invested in these changes, you will want to share this list with someone: a therapist, your teen's therapist, a friend or your spouse. Tell them what your goals are and how they can help you.

teen or the ultimate treatment outcomes. This book will help you to lay open the process and zero in on what you can control and change.

The Ideal Relationship with Your Program
Become a Partner in the Process

As a parent with a special needs child in treatment ("one-foot target" child), you should consider yourself a partner in the process. You aren't doing the work, but you should be involved almost daily, even if it's in a deliberate self-improvement process, with an eye on the day you are to be reunited with your son or daughter. That said, there is a balance that you need to find: As a partner, your thoughts, ideas and input are needed. In some ways you are influencing the direction of therapy. On the other hand, you have hired someone who has expertise and resources in an area that you do not. Your job is also to be the listener and the learner. Too much interference implies you don't really trust what's going on here, and you're going to have to come in and save the day. I urge you to "back off," and instead, take a humble and teachable approach. You've done your homework, hired the best you can, and now you need to let them teach you all they can. Obviously, treatment professionals are going to want to tap into your knowledge base to form their treatment plan for your son or daughter. Well-meaning but ultimately unhealthy or unhelpful input, interruptions or interference (e.g., calling to make sure meds are given, excessively following up on school work, and basically trying to run things from afar) will only slow the process.

Don't Be Laissez-Faire

Beware of slipping into a relationship that could be considered laissez-faire. In the eighteenth century, laissez-faire was used to describe an economic theory of government's noninterference in business. Some parents take this stance with their teen's treatment program. They disconnect and move on with their life with little thought about how their participation would enhance the experience for both themselves and their teen. Some parents disconnect not because they lack interest, but because they are tired, and they believe they have no power or influence on the situation. In either case the parent is forfeiting personal and relational growth opportunities that may never come again. I want you to understand that it's not by chance, or solely through the good work of the professionals, that your teen and family will see the growth and success you are hoping for. There is much you can offer the program staff by way of information, history and insight. Give them all you can to help them get up to speed quickly. Tell them what has worked and what hasn't. Be open about the full family system dynamics so they can zero in on the targets they want to set for treatment of the whole system.

The engagement style you take with the program staff is likely to parallel the style you take with your teen. In that sense, it offers you a "window of insight" into how you tend to interact with your child. The best part about this is that your program therapist will quickly get a feel for what it's like to be your child. And handling that well can become an advantage to you in learning how to change some of the unhelpful aspects of your parenting style.

Be an Engaged Collaborator

The ideal type of parent has a collaborative relationship with the program. This is what I want you to shoot for. This parental attitude is a healthy mix of just enough engagement and just enough restraint to open up the space as well as the structured support to allow the treatment program and your child to work at maximum effectiveness. Let go and allow them to use their expertise on your behalf. These experts have worked with so many teens it doesn't take them long to hone in on the individual issues, relational issues and cognitive issues to target for improvement. They can guide the process from there. No need for panic attacks; this is absolutely possible, even if you haven't been "ideal" in the past. I've seen parents find the right balance over and over again. Moms and dads step up or back off in subtle ways that set off huge ripple effects.

"How should a parent look at treatment in the grand scheme of things? I would look at out-of-home treatment as a catalyst for the change process and that the change process will have to go on long after the program is over. And that a lot of the change is really about learning how to be together in a different way. It's not about any one person changing. It's about starting a process of a lot of hard work and there is probably no better way that I could recommend for some kids and families to start that change process than to have that kind of experience [treatment]. That total separation, rethinking, finding a whole new way of looking at the situation and having that breather to do that in—invaluable." —PARENT, (OREGON)

Ideal program parents do their part by:

- Giving input and working hard on their own assignments;

- Continually listening and learning;

- Refraining from becoming defensive;

- Developing a clear understanding of the plan;

- Valuing the talents and expertise of team members;

- Viewing the problem as a family system's problem, not simply a teen problem;

- Aligning their goals and expectations with the program's.

When I started Homeward Bound, more than one professional admitted to me that some family milieus were so fraught with conflicts, dysfunction and complexity that they would rarely recommend the teen return home. There was a feeling that since there was nothing they could do about the home environment, the best they could do was keep the teen in a safe environment until he or she could transition to some kind of independent living scenario. This ran counter to my desire for teens to be with their families during those important adolescent years, but I understood their concerns; in some families, parents have serious personal challenges that sabotage any progress made by the teen. Such challenges could include addictions, severe depression, suicidal tendencies, verbal or emotional abuse, or having diagnosed or undiagnosed personality disorders. Any of these can make the parent volatile and unpredictable and create a toxic environment at home. The trauma work done in treatment is to help the teens become assertive and take care of themselves in these situations.

This is why I had you do the résumé of failure; it will shine the spotlight on the personal or relationship issues you have that will not only sabotage treatment but doom your teen's progress to failure if you haven't made significant progress before your teen comes home.

I want to discuss some of the extreme traps that most parents won't fall into, but that some parents unwittingly do. I am highlighting these so you can take note, be watchful and highly self-aware to avoid slipping into these destructive patterns. If you do, you will recognize it and jump back out. Remember, I wrote this book because my number-one goal is to help you position yourself to become the X-factor, the significant ingredient, to boost your teen's success in and after treatment, and you can't be that X-factor unless you are at your best.

Treatment Resistant Family Dynamics

Jon Worbets and Victor Houser gave a presentation at a recent national conference I attended on working with three particularly difficult family dynamics in treatment. I knew immediately that they were hitting on some concepts that needed to be included in this book, so I called Jon and discussed the three types of dynamics as they related to the focus of this book. They are:

1. The enmeshed family;

2. The emotionally detached family;

3. The polar and divided family.

Let's look at these types of family dynamics one at a time and pay particular attention to the role the parent plays in these patterns and how they can ultimately undermine treatment success.

The Enmeshed Family

Point to nearly any positive endeavor in life, and we can find examples where it has been taken to the extreme, negatively affecting the extremist's life and those of the people around that person. Consider the innocuous hobby of coin collecting. Given its proper place and scale in life, this hobby is a harmless pastime. However, consider what happens in cases where it's taken to extremes. We see individuals who have very little money to cover their living expenses failing to provide necessities for their children, while having tens of thousands of dollars in rare coins that they refuse to part with. And so it goes with just about anything positive: when taken to extremes, the endeavor becomes negative.

Balance is vitally important in the area of parenting too. For example, it's important that you love and care for your child. But if your whole life revolves around that child, if you stop caring for yourself and lose balance, then bad things happen—not just to you, but to those closest to you as well. As children grow up, they may have parents whose every emotion is somehow connected to them. The parents' identity is eventually fused with that of their children. When the children are upset, the parents are also. They have a hard time separating how their children feel from how they themselves feel. Pretty soon, these children start to feel responsible for their parents' happiness, which becomes a great burden for them. Some of them grow up unable to find the balance between self-care and helping others. Others might grow up angry and resentful that they were put in such a position and can't seem to take responsibility for themselves and their emotions.

What might happen when enmeshed parents have teens in a treatment program? Because those parents identify so strongly with their sons or daughters, they may have great difficulty being objective enough to see the benefits of allowing their teens to struggle through the therapeutic process. The extremely enmeshed may truly feel that their teens can't possibly make it through the challenges of growth, and want to rescue their children to avoid the pain and discomfort of seeing them experience challenges, anger, sadness or failure. Some of these parents may be tempted to pull their teens from treatment early. Unfortunately, these teens become very good at deliberately pushing their parents' buttons to get rescued, with claims of "I can't do this," or "I'm finished. I've learned what I needed to." And not all of these teens are trying to manipulate their parents by lying about their ability to handle the program. If they've been rescued too often in their lives, they will actually believe they can't do it.

Recently, our family got hooked on the reality show *Out of the Wild*. Participants were dropped off in the wilds of a rain forest. As a small group, their mission was to hike back to civilization. They were given very little by way of supplies and had to rely on the group and themselves to survive by finding food, building shelters, doctoring injuries and constantly moving forward. They were also given a radio with a rescue button on it. If they pushed that button, a helicopter would arrive within minutes to rescue them, no questions asked, and they were whisked out of the hardship. Unfortunately, some parents unwittingly provide their teens with a "rescue radio" of their own, preventing their teens from learning new coping skills, acquiring personal awareness or taking on responsibilities. Instead, they reinforce the teens' belief that manipulation or simply calling for help works.

As a wilderness therapist, I worked with one young man from Arizona who would do absolutely nothing each day and defiantly brag that his father's private jet would be landing on the gravel road nearby within a three-day period to take him out of the program. He didn't do a darn thing for two weeks, expecting that his father would soon show up. As you might predict, it took all of my focus in those two weeks to keep the father and his jet parked in Arizona. This became a much more time-consuming and expensive process for the entire family because of the delays in the teen taking personal responsibility for himself and the interference of the father.

> "I can understand and feel what you're feeling right now, but I can't remove that from you. I'm just going to listen to you and be there with you while you go through this challenging time."

The message I want you to send to your teen (in word and deed) is: "I can understand and feel what you're feeling right now, but I can't remove that from you. I'm just going to listen to you and be there with you while you go through this challenging time."

Another story illustrates the problems enmeshment creates at home before treatment. Simon was a young man who had become powerfully addicted to online gaming. He was socially awkward to begin with, so he'd removed himself from any social interaction that created anxiety, and his parents allowed it because his mother felt sorry for him and it hurt her greatly to see him suffer. More and more, he retreated from the real world and lived his life through the computer. He was so committed to playing games at home with his online friends that his mom and dad had completely lost control of him. He refused to go to school and he stayed up all night; he had pretty much checked out of daily life. He didn't care for himself. His hygiene was horrendous, and he was profoundly depressed. But he was stuck in a toxic life pattern that his parents couldn't extricate him from.

Somehow, they managed to get him into the car and brought him out to us at our wilderness program. He was lying in the backseat when they came into the office and said, "Hey, we need some help getting Simon out of the car." Generally, parents will transport their teen to treatment via professionals, but against our counsel, these folks had lied to their son about where they were taking him, and he was furious. (I have heard some parents tell their kid they were going skiing in Utah, or to the Winter Olympics in Salt Lake City in 2002. Don't lie!)

When we went out to the parking lot, he wanted to lash out at me, but he was so weak physically, he couldn't do any damage. After quite some time we were able to talk him into coming in, probably because it was the middle of winter and the car was becoming an icebox. Once we had him dressed and geared up to go, the transporters took him out to the field 50 miles away. Picture it: he went from his basement and the computer where he'd pretty much stayed for the last 3 years, to the wilds of the high mountain deserts of Utah. We had three feet of snow on the ground at the time, and I was very concerned for his safety because he was much worse off than his parents had told us; I saw him as completely incapable of caring for himself.

I told the staff, "Keep a really good eye on him. Make sure he's tucked in and doesn't freeze tonight." And that night, sure enough, they literally had to help him get into his sleeping bag and sleep next to him to keep him safe.

Only two days later, when I arrived in the field to do therapy, I was amazed to see that there was already a visible difference in him. As we were talking, he reached down with his bare hands and picked up the snow, as though the sensory experience of holding something cold was stimulating to him. In the days that followed, I watched as this boy, who'd been taken out of that very toxic, undisciplined place to an environment where his primary activity was to take responsibility for himself, seemed to be born again. It was as though he was coming out of his cocoon of immobility and began interacting with the world for the first time. He was even smiling!

Simon still had a long, long way to go once our wilderness program was done, but that break from his unchallenged online life at home woke him up and brought him out of the near-coma he was in, daily getting stronger physically as well as emotionally. But none of his progress would have mattered if, when he went home, his basement, computer and "virtual life" were waiting for him, or if his parents' emotions continued to be welded to his, making it nearly impossible to watch him struggle with responsibility or difficulty. The easy rut for him to slide into would have been to go back to the computer when life became challenging. The natural rut for his parents would have been that when they saw him relax or brighten up when he went to the computer, they would have allowed him to do so because of the temporary release from tension it would have provided the entire family.

The Emotionally Detached Family

The concept of attachment springs from a theory that parents and their infants bond through behaviors such as smiling, reaching, crying and seeking proximity. If an infant feels secure with its caregiver and that relationship, the infant is freed up to branch out and explore its world.

Research shows that there is another attachment window of opportunity in adolescence for teens to develop socially, relationally and mentally when they feel secure. We may have understood that teens are trying to detach from their parents to develop new friendships or romantic partners. What this study found was that a successful transition from adolescence isn't about detaching, but about maintaining a secure attachment and emotional connectedness with parents while becoming more independent (Moretti, 2004).

Parents can become emotionally detached from their child for a number of reasons. Often, they have their own personal mental health issues, acute life stressors, substance abuse or other addictions that keep them from frequently or deeply connecting with their teen. It's very common that the things that create disconnect with their children are hidden and kept as secrets. Sometimes the parents are simply too busy and choose to devote their attention to careers, hobbies, romantic relationships, and so on, rather than prioritize relationships with their family or their role in the treatment process. At other times it's a continuation of

> The message you want to send to your teen (in word and deed) is: "I know I haven't been there for you in the past. And I'm not sure how to be there for you now and in the future. But I want you to know that I'm going to work hard to figure that out, no matter how painful that is for me."

family patterns from the previous generation, when the parent also grew up with a detached parent and so has a hard time envisioning what a healthy, connected family looks like.

Whatever the cause of the detachment may be, a lack of connection to the teen generally causes acting out and mental health issues for the teen. Good treatment programs try to address the issues that are creating a wedge between the parent and adolescent by offering new ways for them to talk, work and play again. Though we logically "get this," this is where things become uncomfortable for us, as parents, knowing that our own issues and challenges must be addressed for the sake of our teen's progress.

> If you aren't being personally challenged during your teen's treatment, you are paying too much for the treatment program.

Do you see what a difficult situation this creates in a treatment program and for your program therapist? You, the paying client, are now being asked to stretch and change your relationship with your adolescent. This might require that you address something that you are not proud of, a big family secret, or at the very least some touchy topics. And you are paying for this? Herein lies one of the great dilemmas of a healer: Our goal is to help people feel better and do better, but that often requires people to *become* better. Becoming better is often stressful, if not out and out painful. But good programs won't shy away from this. Their job—actually, their mission—is to help the teen heal, grow, mature and become a healthy, happy person, and they must bring the parent into the equation and treatment process to do so. Hear me when I say this: *If you aren't being personally challenged during your teen's treatment, you are paying too much for the treatment program.*

The Polar and Divided Family

When you hear the term *polar and divided family* you may be picturing a divorce scenario, but there are as many intact families that suffer from this syndrome. For example, let's say a couple has a history of division and disagreement over a great many issues and their child's placement in a program is yet one more point of conflict. Dad may feel angry and think the daughter didn't need or deserve admission into a treatment program and hence won't support it. The more Mom engages and tries to move things forward with the professionals she's been working with as the "willing client," the more resentful and out of the loop Dad becomes. Consequently the treatment of the teen and the progress of the family system are greatly affected, if not stopped all together. These conflicts are hard to conceal and will still come across to the teen loud and clear, even through written letters. Even if teens are absent from home, they will assume the division remains. How could it be otherwise? They have witnessed years of the conflicting styles and until there is repeated hard evidence to the contrary, that old dynamic shapes treatment adversely.

Some parents will at times experience wide polar swings, moving from being highly engaged to being almost completely cut off. These swings might be totally dictated by their own addictions or mental health issues. Parents caught up in this pattern can be "on board" one day, but the next day finds them irrational and blaming, unable or unwilling to cooperate with the program or the other parent.

Laura

Laura was functional—barely—but because of the conflict she had with her ex-husband and their four children, she would go into bouts of depression and paranoia that left her incapable of creating any kind of safety and consistency in her home life. She lost her job, she alienated the extended family who tried to help and she completely wore out any friend or professional who would attempt to listen to and support her. When she did interact with her kids, she either sent messages that their father was a loser, or blamed her kids' bad behavior for the chaos in their lives. Her extreme mental health issues were just as debilitating as any addiction. When in the grip of depression, she was known to pull away into her own world, without energy or resources to offer her kids. The children felt isolated and unsure of their mom's love. Therefore they struggled mightily to grow and mature because they were so concerned about the fundamental relationship with their mother. During those disconnected times there was no structure, nor were there any boundaries in the home, so the children became accustomed to doing whatever they wanted. When their mother tried to reassert her leadership, it was completely ineffective, which drove her into further depression and blaming.

> The message you want to send your teen (in word and deed): "We love you enough to overcome our own challenges so we can be there for you. I'm so sorry for the pain our divided parenting ... our inconsistency ... and so on, has caused you."

The fact is parents must address their own issues before they can effectively put their love for their teen on center stage. Doing so gives them a reason to overcome illness, hurt, pride and differences. I've always enjoyed the *Reader's Digest* stories of "Drama in Real Life" that tell of miracles performed by parents who, themselves on the edge of death, do heroic things to save a child they love. This is no different, and it may take that kind of love and that kind of superhuman strength in your situation as well.

The message you want to send your teen (in word and deed): "We love you enough to overcome our own challenges so we can be there for you. I'm so sorry for the pain our divided parenting ... our inconsistency ... and so on, has caused you."

Stages in the Parent/Program Partnership

There are stages and principles to being an educated and effective partner in the process of your teen's therapeutic treatment: let go, brace yourself for manipulation, re-engage, remodel the relationship and make a game plan. Let me elaborate.

Letting Go

As parents, we are charged with the care of precious human beings. We feed them, clothe them, play with them, counsel them, provide them with opportunities and love them. We are never on vacation; the responsibility follows us everywhere. For some parents the last decade and a half has been spent managing, advocating and fixing things for their child. In extreme cases in which the young person's disabilities or issues have been both acute and chronic, the caregiver's identity is often swallowed up in the role. Out-of-home treatment in such cases is going to feel extremely uncomfortable for these parents, yet at the same time, it will be a massive relief to have the decision made and others brought in to help. Now, those parents' job is to learn to "let go." This is challenging because in most cases, they have been managing every aspect of that teen's life as best they could through each new crisis.

The healing process is not an event; it takes time. Parents need to take a deep breath and trust that the program can contain their teen in a safe way and start to create that supportive environment for them. You were careful—and most likely prayerful—in the choice of the program, so now you need to take a mini-vacation from the stress and responsibility you have been carrying.

Imagine that you want to hire a contractor to build an addition onto your home. You would have interviewed several professionals, called references and looked at their previous work. Once you settled on the right builder for the job, how do you think they would be most effective? It would slow down and frustrate everyone if, every time they sawed through a board, you were there underfoot with your little whisk broom, sweeping up the mess, and neatly rearranging the tools. What you see as helpful may actually be impeding the process.

In the first few days and weeks of treatment, your child needs to let go and settle in too. He can do that so much better if he can observe your example of letting go first. Of course, you are still the parent, and if you have questions, you should be able to ask those of the program staff so you can understand why they do certain things. Just remember that you generally can't improve their clinical processes. They've done this hundreds of times before and all you'll do is send the wrong message—one that says you don't trust what's happening. This is poison to the process.

Here are some suggestions for the best use of your program and hometown professional team so you can confidently and safely "let go."

1. Talk to your educational consultants about what they've seen in the dozens of programs they refer families to. They can tell you if your concerns are normal or warranted.

2. Keep your hometown physicians in the loop so they can use their experience with your teen's health history to recommend medications or advise the program on health issues.

3. If you haven't already done so, let your teen's school staff know where your teen is, and what the goals of the treatment are. If they are in on the process, they will be much more helpful in the reintegration should your son or daughter return to that school.

4. The program therapist is going to be your best friend in the coming weeks or months. He or she is the messenger who will report what is occurring during the week with school, activities, chores and therapy sessions. Most therapists are excellent communicators, so keep those lines of communication flowing both ways.

Brace Yourself

"Brace myself for what?" you might ask. Anticipate that your teen is going to make at least one attempt to manipulate you into taking him or her out of the program as fast as possible. He or she will do this in lots of different ways. I've seen kids write letters to their parents that would just terrify you. I've heard examples where they'll tell their parents that their lives are in danger: the other kids in the program are trying to hurt or kill them, or the staff are abusive—any number of things. They may go on a hunger strike. I've seen them try to split their parents up via letters, because pitting their parents against each other worked before they left home, so if they can get the soft one to see how bad life is for them, then the soft one might be able to talk the strict one out of sticking with the plan.

Recently, I was coaching a family at the same time their son entered a treatment program. They received a letter that typifies the tactics that I'm talking about. Prior to getting their son's letter, their program therapist, Scott Jones, wrote them an e-mail and expertly explained it this way:

I have attached your first letter from Jordan, which he wrote yesterday. You will see from it that he is frustrated and trying to get you to rescue him. Most adolescents, confronted with a novel setting, will run through their repertoire of coping strategies—anger, manipulation, withdrawal, etc. Some of the most common strategies I see from new students include:

- Threats—"If you don't get me out of here, you'll never see your grandchildren."

- Regrets—"I'm sorry for all the pain I've caused you. I have learned my lesson."

- Promises—"I will do..."

- Manipulation —"I need to be home so we can work on our issues together."

- Confidence Undermining: —"I'm not like any of these kids in the program." Or "This is the worst program ever, a total waste."

You will probably recognize a few of these in Jordan's letter.

My advice? Write back to him, reaffirm your love and confidence in his ability to work through this tough time and trust the process.

My wife has a group of women who speedwalk distance races together. When muscle fatigue or chaffing sets in, one woman will say, "Hello pain ... I've been expecting you." They laugh and the mood shifts. So when you get a communication that echoes some of what was listed above, do not let it take your legs out from under you. I want you to make this your mantra: "Hello, resistance (rescue pleas, manipulation, etc.) ... I've been expecting you." Recognize it for what it is and know that this is far from the first time your program staff have dealt with this. They understand how traumatic the separation and transition are and they know how to move through this phase and resistance. They are expert at helping teens work through their fear, anger or discomfort to use this experience for their benefit. Teens will eventually begin to think, "Hey, maybe splitting Mom and Dad is not going to work anymore. It's not getting me pulled from the program. Maybe I'd better get with the program myself, let go of these old tactics I've used to cope with life, and try something new."

Think back to a few months after this child joined your family. You might have thought, "Alright! I'm getting the hang of this parenting thing. It's doable." About five years later, you were settling in much better and *now* you had your hands around what it took. You may be chuckling to yourself here because the whole parenting onion just keeps going deeper, layer after layer, and some far-off day you hope to reach the core understanding of parenting. You are in good company, my friends. We all feel that way. Treatment will take the same kind of unfolding process for your teen to really understand his or her own feelings and the consequences of his or her behavior or choices.

Though in the beginning you are anxious about your teen's emotional ups and downs, low self-esteem or opposition to authority figures, you need to relax. Many teens may truly believe they can't do hard things, so when they plead for help, it's sincere. But the reality is they will be able to make it, and they need your confidence in that ability. I have heard it said by multiple treatment professionals that the goal is to teach parents that they need to prepare the child for the path rather than prepare the path for the child. Our world demands certain things from a person to be successful. You can't force the world to conform to the child, so you must help the child gain the skills to function well in the world. Parents, particularly of a special needs child, understandably get into the habit of making accommodations and smoothing the path for that child. Sometimes this is taken too far. The "solution" becomes the problem. Another mantra for you: "Prepare the child, not the path."

Believe me, I understand how hard it is to get kids to accept the fact that they are capable of hard things. An article I read in *Success* magazine suggested that a person look around the walls of his office to see what it is that he values. Are golf trophies, family photos, antiques or world maps posted on those walls? What is it that you are teaching others about what you value? We had to laugh when looking around our office; I have two paintings by a local artist, one of a man using a team of horses to cut hay, and the other of a family throwing out hay to cattle in a snowy field. The wall calendar is a freebie from a local feed company of Western art depicting cowboys at work. The brass civil-war cannon is a reminder of what was sacrificed for freedom. Basically, we are trying to teach our kids, via osmosis, that sacrifice and hard work are an expectation and part of the Thayne makeup. We even went so far as to buy a hog farm to make sure they got the message. It's a work in progress; some of the kids are taking to the

> "Prepare the child, not the path."

idea quite nicely, while others mope and complain and don't want to work on the farm unless they can bring a friend.

I was raised by a father who not only believed that I could do hard things but expected it. When I was 16 years old, Dad had too many excavation jobs to do by a certain deadline. So he took me over to a neighboring farmer who needed an irrigation system put in. He dropped me off with one of his Case backhoes, had me go meet with the farmer to see what he needed, and left me to dig the trench with the parting advice, "Don't hit any other lines!" Another job found me up on the Dry Gulch Irrigation ditch that wound around the steep edge of a hill in Duchesne Utah. The hill side sloped off at a steep 60 degree angle and the bank was only wide enough for my two outside tires to rest on. I ran the machines inside tires in the ditch itself. My job was to deepen and widen the half-mile ditch out without rolling end-over-end off the hill, killing myself and destroying a very expensive piece of equipment. These jobs, as you might guess, stretched me right to the point of my capabilities, and in some cases beyond. But I am grateful now for my dad's belief in me and his providing me the opportunity to learn to believe in myself.

With that said, remember to allow the process to work, and teach your young people they can survive and succeed. Instead of siding with them against the program or against the other parent, just listen empathetically to them but express confidence in their being able to find the strength they need to cope with the new situation, to learn what they need to learn and to understand how they got themselves into the hole they're in. Leave it on their plate. Don't second guess your decision for seeking treatment. If you do that, you'll end up undermining the program and their progress. Teens will sit tight and wait to see if you're going to swoop in and rescue them. If, for any reason, you do feel unsafe, consult your professionals until you feel at ease. Communicate your concerns but do it with an open mind to learn how they handle the situations that you're troubled about.

In addition to joining the program in the beginning, there are going to be many other times along your journey that you will need to support the policies and practices of the program, even if it's different from what you've been doing in your own home.

Re-engage

I saw it in the faces of Will and Nancy. They were exhausted. Dad had had it with their 16-year-old, Tanner. Mom was distraught and wanted to forgive and find an alternative to out-of-home placement. They had come to me looking for options, not only for this son, but for their whole family. He wasn't a bad kid; he was just rapidly heading down a path that led to nowhere good. He was smoking marijuana daily, failing in his classes, and disengaging from his family. This family had money, and were beating themselves up about having given too much to their children, with too few expectations. When they decided to place their boy in a wilderness program, they felt a huge weight fall off their shoulders. They realized they had been depressed and worried constantly for the last year, and now they could turn over the responsibility and brain power it took to keep him safe for a time.

> *I could see that our way of interacting with him and parenting wasn't working because we were so angry all the time. I really didn't have a sense of how to change the game and start to parent him better. I think I was hoping that he could have a breather while he was away getting some experiences away from home and us. And with us having a breather to be able to regroup and*

look at the situation with fresh eyes, all of us would come back
with a new perspective. —PARENTS (SOUTH CAROLINA)

As with all families, I gave Will and Nancy permission to relish the peace and break. They could pick up a hobby they had to set aside when things started going south, or maybe even get away together for a while. The downtime would rest and rejuvenate them, enabling them to join in with new perspectives, energy and determination to play their role in the treatment process like stars. The one warning I had for them, and for you, was to take a breather but DO NOT DISENGAGE. Rest but don't fall off your teen's radar.

Isaiah

If this sounds like a no-brainer, believe me there are plenty of parents that will not re-engage once the admissions paperwork is complete. They're simply too sick, mad, hurt, exhausted or distracted. Isaiah was from a family such as this. He had pushed every frustration and panic button on his parents for so long that by the time they finished wilderness therapy, the last thing they wanted to do was get back to work with him at home. The mom was physically in bad shape and struggling with illness. His father was distracted by phone calls the whole time I met with them. I was pulling for the family's success more than they were. I tried every tactic to engage, threaten and beg for their participation, but they wanted to just pay me to do what I did and leave them out of it. Well, that's not the kind of work I do. I've tried it before with extremely disappointing results, therefore, we decided not to work together. Please, don't be this kind of parent.

After a short emotional break from the situation, it's time to join up with the program, and there are many ways for you to do that. Program staff understand that parent engagement is vital in long-term success, just as the research shows. They have developed different components of their program to involve the parents. For example, family therapy might be weekly or every other week. Though you may be tempted to only ask for a simple update or to talk to your teen during that therapy hour, be sure to tell your therapist you are ready to work and want to use your time effectively.

Parent workshops are held every few months to train the family on campus. Meet the staff, eat the food and connect with other parents and students to have a visual of the people your teen is talking about. Get a feel for the culture and allow time for your teen to "show off" a little. Get curious about the process and daily activities. Your teen is working hard and looking to you for interest and approval.

These visits are not just a chance to spend time with your teen. You are in classes that teach you skills for parenting a teen with challenges. Groups on different topics come together so you can understand the diagnosis better—for example, learning about body image or trauma, or having experiential exercises such as a ropes course or river rafting trip. One of the fringe benefits of these parent days is that you will meet other parents and form relationships that support you in ways nothing else can. The parents who are ultimately successful after treatment have made it their quest to make changes in tandem with their teen's changes. An important aspect to making change is in our next point.

Remodel the Relationship

Treatment affords you the opportunity to fundamentally change the dynamics between you and your teen, not simply warm up the relationship again. Think of this as a chance to do a remodel just as you have probably done in the past with your home. As in the case of a home remodel, restoring the relationship with your son or daughter is much more pleasant and efficient when you are living away from the construction zone.

Aim high and shoot to have your relationship look, feel and function differently by the time your teen is finished with treatment. While I can't tell you what will need to change in your relationship, it's safe to assume that it isn't working as well as it could be right now and that there is definite room for improvement. Fortunately treatment provides the space for it.

Starting over and healing the relationship with your son or daughter, or closing the distance, is more possible in a treatment setting than if you were in perpetual conflict at home, or in a cycle of avoidance. Tensions will subside. Communication is often slowed down and limited to letter writing for the first few weeks. This may sound counterintuitive (e.g., isn't communication the means for a child and parent to work through issues and come closer together?), but parents have frequently reported that they have fond memories of the time they were writing to and receiving letters from their teen. They tell us that although they felt that the communication back and forth was unnatural and painfully slow, they also recognized that it freed them from being "live," which often takes the form of the ineffective and habitual back-and-forth, rapid-fire communication that defined their interactions prior to treatment. You might wonder why they would have a policy on communication that feels so unnatural. Doing that which comes naturally is simply compounding the problem.

Letters, calls and visits offer vehicles for clarifying your contributions to the issues, allowing you time to apologize sincerely. How long has it been since you have done so and asked for forgiveness? There is such power to melt hearts and years of resentment when you can say you are sorry. Whether your teen chooses to accept that or not is not your responsibility. Keep your eye on yourself. These vehicles also afford the opportunity to state what you would like to see more of in your relationship or home. You are essentially creating a version of your life together. You are stating your views with a solid understanding born from a rocky history of what you commit to creating in your future.

A good parent-teen relationship generally has these qualities:

- Mutual honesty;

- Stick-to-itiveness when things become tough and you'd like to abandon a situation;

- Your teen's acceptance of responsibility for his or her own contribution to the problem;

- Remorse for harm done;

- Shared love and appreciation for efforts and strengths;

- Mutual respect;

- Good humor and fun;

- Parent/child or teen relationship (not best friend/teen)

Lead by Example

Programs cannot force change on your teen or on you. They will put elements in place to *invite* change, but teens will do so on their own timeline. Some parents have the mindset that they are purchasing an outcome, when in reality they are purchasing a process that stacks the deck in favor of that outcome.

What's good for the goose is good for the gander. Mary Alexine, founder of a girl's residential program reminds us, "Parents must recognize their own process of change. It's not that residential or wilderness programs are magic; it's hard work for everyone. The learning curve is steep for the student, but parents are required to start doing things differently as well."

Dylan

One story of leading by example, which may be a slightly extreme one, is about the mother of a young man named Dylan. He was in my boys' group at Outback Therapeutic Expeditions. He refused to do anything. We required teens to build their own fires using a primitive tool called a bow-drill fire set. Until they could build a fire, they ate their food cold. They got to eat what they wanted from what we provided, but they couldn't cook it on somebody else's fire. This rule really motivated them to get with the program and learn to do it. There were some kids who in the end lacked hand-eye coordination and genuinely couldn't learn, and of course we made accommodations for them. But this boy had no such challenges; he simply refused, telling me day after day that his mom was going to come and get him out of the program. I kept assuring him, "Your mom is not going to come get you out of the program. You need to do this and I'm willing to help you, but you've got to help yourself. I can't do it all for you."

But he just believed so deeply down in his bones that she would take him out of there that he literally went for weeks without doing anything toward building his own fire, or many other things for that matter. He would hike with us and get to the camps but kept eating cold food. He was marking time until she got there.

I knew that it was actually highly likely she would want to pull him out and take him home, because she was so convinced that her child really couldn't do things and was concerned for his safety (a classic case of enmeshed parenting that I spoke about earlier). Consequently I asked her not to come out unless she was willing to follow my instructions exactly, and that might mean not being able to talk to her son. It might mean that she simply came in, watched him from a distance all day long and went home without speaking to him.

She agreed to do that and she flew out. I gave her a big pep talk before we drove to the field, knowing that her powerful motherly instincts and old patterns would kick in and she'd want to rescue Dylan. We went out to the field where he was camping with his group and I had her stay in the car while I went in and talked to the field staff. Upon reaching the staff, I asked them whether Dylan had built a fire yet. "No, he just barely got out of his sleeping bag this morning. We've been trying to motivate him, but he is still refusing to work on a fire" they said. I was disappointed....but not surprised. I said, "We're going to try something radical today. This is going to be hard so buckle up. I'm going to have his mother sit about 30 yards from his solo campsite. Before doing so though I will talk to Dylan and let him know that if he wants to talk to her, he has to build a fire for her and then we can invite her in to sit around the campfire with him."

I talked with the mother and reminded her, "If you talk to your son before he accomplishes this, I'm going to have to ask you to leave. I would really hate to do that so please make a firm commitment not to speak with him." As hard as that was for her, she agreed to it. I shared the game plan with Dylan and explained that if he talked to his mother and she spoke back to him, she would have to leave, so I urged him not to tempt her—"But instead of that, let's focus on helping you start a fire." He'd seen many fires built over that time and I asked him, "How's your fire set? What do you have?" He didn't have a spindle or a top rock. His fireboard was only partially flattened from whittling; unfinished. The bow was a bent stick, not long enough to do any good. We were basically starting from scratch. Questions ran through my head; how committed am I to this? How committed is his mother? And how committed is Dylan? I resolved again that I was all in and that might help the others do the same.

I said, "I'm going to have a field staff member here with you and they're going to help you build a good set, but the first thing you have to do is go out and find the materials." Mom came and sat in her lawn chair, watching him. He refused to do anything for a little while. He just kind of sat there looking at her, and the staff sat there with him. He looked sad. My guess is that he looked sadder than he had ever looked; he was using his mind to will his mother to come to him. It was a torturous hour and a half before he realized that Mom was not going to come to his rescue. Finally, he got up and went hunting for the materials he needed for his bow-drill fire set.

Eventually, while still dragging his feet, he collected the wood needed to craft a fire set. His efforts to build a fire set were so half-hearted that this drug on for hours and hours that day. It was literally late afternoon when he finally came back with a fire set that had a snowball's chance of actually working. The tension was excruciating for all of us. Then, he had to try to start the fire. I can't tell you how difficult this was for me, let alone Mom and the field staff and the boy. It was an enormously challenging day.

Finally, at about four in the afternoon, after several failed attempts, he was finally working hard. A spark of hope; he was really engaged; he was paying attention to his technique; and he was putting his top effort in. He'd painstakingly prepared a little nest of filaments—and I could see that he was creating an ember that was producing smoke. Where there's smoke there's FIRE so I hurriedly motioned for his mom to come to him. As she silently crept up so that she did not distract him, he was blowing this ember into the nest and suddenly, dramatically the nest flamed up. All of the staff and the boys in the camp were tuned in to the drama unfolding, even as they were going about their work. Shrieks of joy and excitement originating from his mother and me, soon could be heard throughout camp; all of us were celebrating. It was an absolutely huge breakthrough for both Mom and Dylan. What came next was a true celebration around the fire for the rest of the evening—and more importantly, a real change in her paradigm about what he could do, and what his true upsides and potential were. Belief, trust, and commitment on his mother's part, led to this magical breakthrough. I couldn't give her enough credit afterward for being willing to go through such a heart-wrenching day. She reported it was "worth it". Subsequently, Dylan's mother never saw him quite the same from that day on.

So, lead by your example. Your son or daughter will be motivated by your leadership. Keep yourself focused on your part and show your child the way.

Make a Game Plan

Adele's son was an addict. While he was in treatment, she faithfully attended group therapy for family members of addicts. She also found her own individual therapist, to work on her anger about her divorce and single parenting responsibilities. That process helped her to become absolutely firm in her belief that she was not serving her son if she allowed him to stay in her home if he began using drugs again. She steadily freed herself from faulty beliefs that held her captive to continually taking care of and feeling responsible for him even when he was not willing to do his part. It helped her move out of the codependent relationship she was in. Adele would tell you that without this therapeutic help, she would have felt it was her duty as a mother to provide the basics of shelter and financial support, regardless of what he was doing on his end, and I have no doubt that his orientation

> **I'm consistently encouraged in this work by parents with the courage to love *differently* from how they have previously.**

toward drug use would have sabotaged the whole outcome. Fortunately for both of them, her firm commitment to not letting him stay with her if he returned to drug use was communicated to him many times during the last few months of treatment and he knew she was serious. She had come to terms with the fact that her parenting style would only lead to the same mess, so she was ready to do the hard things. I'm consistently encouraged in this work by parents with the courage to love *differently* from how they have previously.

Drawing on outsider's perspectives, be they other parents or your therapist, is all part of fortifying yourself with the skills, the emotional management and the commitment to be able to consistently hit that "one-foot target." Find a therapist or parent coach who can think systemically. Find someone you are willing to take coaching from when he or she accurately assesses what you are doing to unwittingly contribute to the problems. That person needs to be a team player, with the ability to collaborate and coordinate his or her efforts with the efforts and direction being taking in the treatment program. Having all professionals pulling in the same direction is essential.

Get Unified with Your Co-parent

Kyle and Brenda had recently gone through a very difficult divorce. There was ongoing fighting, extending all the way to mutual lawsuits. As an executive from Georgia, he had done some things that had violated the trust of his then-wife and children. It had been many years since the family crises he had put them all through, and he had since remarried. Now it was time for their son to come home after treatment and they were both afraid of potential relapse. This fear enabled them to consider working together again for their son's sake, so they hired me to come to their homes and support them in the transition.

We started with a few joint phone calls during which I coached them as they made tentative progress. Within a fairly short period of time they were ready to have me come and facilitate the work in both of their homes. The day I arrived in their town and made my way to Brenda's home, Kyle followed me in. He hadn't been in her home since their divorce four years earlier. I facilitated communication and helped them move past not trusting each other. To Kyle's credit, he took responsibility—for the first time—for the hurt he had caused, and to Brenda's credit, she opened up her heart to forgive him. From there they were able to come together as a team on behalf of their son. As I walked out with Kyle after three days together, he said, "If nothing else positive happens over the next few months, we will be working together; that was already worth every penny. What took place these last few days was nothing short of a miracle." He explained that they had built up a little friendship again, and the freeze between them had thawed sufficiently to let them unite in this effort. The focus was no longer on the problems between the two of them, but on resisting the triangulation with their son. It was now *them* against the struggles their son would go through, rather than viewing one another as the problem. Once again they had two backs to share the burden between. Everything felt lighter once each had the hope that the other co-parent would provide back-up. Though this story took place after treatment, imagine what would have been accomplished if Kyle and Brenda had been unified throughout treatment. Unfortunately, their division had hindered their son's progress in the program, as they would not agree on anything throughout the process. Only one would attend the workshops if they found the other there. Both were tempted to side with their son against the parent or program at different times. If you haven't been united in the past, make unity in your parenting approach paramount on your list. Even if your child turns 18 and is not coming back to either one of your homes, this is still key to your child's long-term success and the quality of your relationships over the years to come.

You remember playing Red Rover in elementary school, don't you? You'd divide into two teams and form two lines facing one another, holding hands with the child next to you. One side would chant, "Red Rover, Red Rover, send Sally right over." Then Sally would come running to try to break through the line. If she wasn't successful, she would have to join the opposing team. If she was successful, she took one of the other team's people back to her side.

Teens need to see such a strong front waiting that no amount of effort would break the bonds of unity between their parents. That knowledge invites them to give up wasting precious time and energy in pitting Mom against Dad (or step-parent, or grandparent or program) and allows them to focus on their own work. This results in all three parties getting on the same team.

Grab your highlighter, because this piece is critical. Separation and divorce can be a very bitter thing, and sometimes it's everything a parent can do not to undermine the other parent. I get that. But no matter what your differences are, or how toxic your history together has been, the common denominator you have is that child. Please recognize that the united front is for the child, not for the person you were married to. That should be motivation enough to help you swallow your pride, put aside the zingers you want to let fly, and concentrate on being a good *co-parent*. Obviously, if you have a wonderful relationship with the other co-parent, whether you're married or not, that's even better. But at the very least, there has got to be cooperation. I have seen boulder-sized animosity shrink to the size of a pea almost overnight as a result of one person's humility and willingness to change and forgive.

> **The united front is for the child, not for the person you were married to.**

Full parental involvement means that you go together to parent days. If you're divorced and it's awkward, know that you're also going to get a lot of support. You will meet many other parents who are in the same boat with their co-parents. You might start the day at the workshop feeling extremely uncomfortable, but as the day progressed, things will smooth out. You will begin to see how you can work together again. Step-parents will sometimes feel uncomfortable in this equation, but often they can be an important part of the overall plan and can offer some outsider perspective. Use your best judgment on their involvement. Use the months when your teen is away to work on your co-parenting skills, when you aren't dealing with real-time crises in your teen's life. Practice better communication during the lull. If you weren't initially in favor of the treatment program and went along unwillingly, accept that the decision has been made and join up and let your teen know you're behind

> Use the months when your teen is away to work on your co-parenting skills, when you aren't dealing with real-time crises in your teen's life.

it. You'll feel a lot better, your co-parent will be stunned, and your teen will improve more quickly. As you persist in leading by compromising with your co-parent, you will see your co-parent change. I can't promise how much your co-parent will change or in what direction. The level of mistrust might be so great that your co-parent holds onto the skepticism for months. But it's a virtual certainty, based on the laws of human interaction, that if you change yourself for the right reasons (not to manipulate your co-parent), your co-parent will change too. Remember, it takes two people to maintain a cycle and therefore only one to break it. Discuss openly with your co-parent your mutual vision for your teen and for your co-parenting relationship. Identify your mutual expectations of your son or daughter as a basis for a co-parenting plan for the future. Clarity is essential here as you try to predict what will happen at home with friends, schools, visitation, and so on. The use of a parent coach to find common ground and work-arounds where there are disagreements can be hugely beneficial.

If you are alone in this—if there is no co-parent—obviously the unity factor is not an issue but *your* stress comes in the form of greater demands on your stamina. The event that led to your being alone probably added to the trauma in the home likely affecting both you and your teen. Being alone magnifies your need to connect with other parents who know what you are experiencing and can lend an ear or a solid shoulder to lean on. Yours is the toughest job in parenting.

Appraise the Home Environment

Our work at Homeward Bound is largely focused on helping teens and families make the transition from treatment to home successfully. We have developed a model for doing that. One feature of our model is to visit the home shortly after the teen arrives. Among other things, this gives us a chance to use all of our senses to understand and get a feel for the home, the family and each individual in the environment. We sense the nuances of the family culture and mores as well. You could say we are immersing ourselves in the family "milieu".

If you could look at your home and family culture through my eyes, as a transition coach, what would you see? You would immediately take in the physical layout of the home and neighborhood. I'm not talking about the number of bedrooms and level of housekeeping, as some may worry, but about the rooms where the family gathers. You also have a first impression of the people you meet, some for the first time. Mannerisms are revealed from moment one and are revealed layer by layer throughout the three-day visit. You would take in the physical qualities of the home including the layout of the rooms, places where people congregate, and the use and priority of technology by family members. You would also get a feel for the home's culture. Some homes are very formal and stuffy; others are just the opposite. Some family cultures are laid back and go with the flow and others are go, go, go all the time. Each little detail tells a part of the story.

When members of the family interact, a great deal of data is shared. Relationships, coalitions and hierarchy are exposed regardless of any attempt to conceal them. "It is what it is," as the saying goes. I've been asked many times before, "What if we are on our best behavior when you come? Will this be a waste of your time?" My answer is that every family system has its limits and these limits and patterns always show themselves. A family can put on a show for only so long. Very quickly the surroundings, relationships and dynamics take over and pull them into their common ways of being.

Soon after Jack's son came home from treatment, I was in his California home and we were defining and setting the structure of the home, discussing what kind of home and family life the family would like to have. My side discussions with his parents revealed that both desperately wanted to improve their marriage and wanted to be better examples to their children. The time we spent together seemed to open their eyes to what was possible, and they enthusiastically talked about important principles that would help them guide their children. Jack was inspired by it all and soon we came to the part in our process where we put everything down on paper. We call this the Plan for Moving Forward, or the Family Rules and Consequences. I gave them a template that gives parents a good place to start. Their job was to modify it to fit their own situation and values. We came to the section that included the expectation that their children would not use profanity or vulgarity in the home. This was on the third day I spent in their home, by which time I had heard Jack do a lot of swearing. He regularly flipped his son off in a teasing way, which his wife sorely disapproved of. So I asked him, "Do you want to keep this clause in here?"

He said, "Oh absolutely, I want to keep it in." He was going to toe a hard line with his son.

I raised my eyebrows a bit and looked him in the eye and said, "Now you understand that if you keep this in, you have to live up to these standards yourself, right?"

He looked at me and paused for a second, realizing what I was asking him to do—and he said, "Yeah ... leave it in; it needs to stay." His wife looked at me and smiled. This was a minor miracle for her. Jack seemed to realize the weight of responsibility he had as the father of the home to set an example, in more ways than just his language. He hadn't felt this way for a long time. Jack knew this meant he had to clean up his own language and his own life if he expected his son to do the same.

The kinds of internal changes that need to occur may require out-patient therapy, marriage therapy or even addiction recovery. They can require gaining anger management skills to allow you to solve future problems. It might require identifying your triggers so you can predict and avoid those triggers in the future. Listen to your therapist, or a loved one or your conscience and determine the changes you will make personally. Make them now and you'll inspire others around you to join in the virtuous cycle of change that you are creating in your home.

Marla Cillus, known as the Fly Lady, has a huge following for her book and website on home organization and cleaning. She talks about the CHAOS (can't have anyone over syndrome) she lived in for years until her finances, mental health and marriage fell apart. Baby step by baby step, she pulled herself together and leads her readers on the doable journey from a place of disaster to a home that is a heaven for families.

Put down the book and take a look around your room. What do you see? Are there areas where it is comfortable to gather? Does anyone else besides you use the space? Now expand out to the rest of the house. Are there areas that are being ignored, areas you rarely enter or use because they aren't inviting, have been taken over by your teenagers, or have lost their function? Think of the kitchen. Is it a place where you share meals and stories about your lives, or is it basically a drive-thru refueling station. Think of your teen's bedroom. What is on the walls or on the shelves? What potential distractions are there? Are you living in some of your own CHAOS? What small changes could you make to create a better living environment? Imagine taking everything out of the house and onto the front lawn and then carefully choosing what will be allowed back inside. This is what you are doing when you separate during treatment. Again, you are using the opportunity your child's crisis presents to make deliberate, constructive changes for everyone in the home.

One family in Michigan went so far as to remodel the main living area of their home before their son came back from a short-term equine ranch program. Holes in the walls where he had punched them had to be patched and painted over. There was some swapping of bedrooms between the siblings so that he could be closer to the parents' bedroom. The computer was moved off his bedroom desk and into the family room to help him recover from his gaming and pornography addiction. The parents were deliberate in sending the message that "This is going to be a new home when you get here. We are going to clean house and make it different." Changes like these send an unmistakable message to your teen—though your teen may

Here are some ideas for maintaining your stamina and engagement:

- Read books, like this one, that are concrete, specific, and hopeful.

- Attend support groups or parent days, participate and give back to others.

- Do your homework between sessions with your program therapist.

- Don't miss appointments with your therapist; keep that time sacred.

- Acknowledge and celebrate growth both in yourself and in your teen, because excitement and satisfaction are healthy and desirable parts of change.

- Journal about your experience along the way, so you can go back and review

- Use travel time to and from the program to set goals with your co-parent

not readily appreciate all the changes—as soon as he or she walks in the door.

Evaluate the Academic Environment

Creating a solid plan may also mean a change of academic environment. I'm not saying you need to yank your teen from his or her neighborhood school, but now is the time to start interviewing and investigating all of the options. Home school, charter schools, online programs, alternative high schools and other combinations weren't available even ten years ago but can prove to be a great, flexible advantage for your son or daughter. I'll often use tutors or academic coaches to help families during and following treatment look at tutoring for credit recovery, on-time graduation, college entrance exam prep, executive functioning skills, and so on. They also help parents in speaking with school counselors, tracking transference of credits from treatment program schools, and continuing academic support. With all you are doing to schedule, organize and help prioritize home life, it's a big relief to have someone tasked with watching the academic aspect of your teen's life. Ask your educational consultant to guide you on the needed resources.

Plan for Your Staying Power

How are you feeling right now? Are you reading the above information and stories and feeling overwhelmed? Stop it. This book is not mean to be read straight through like a novel. Pick it up, find something you want to put more thought into and then put it down and act on that thought. Discuss it with your co-parent, write about it, make a task list, a mind map, a spread sheet or whatever you do to help you make a goal and move toward attaining it. Whatever you do, do not forget to nurture yourself along the way. Yes, this might include scheduling a massage or pedicure, or taking time to exercise and get some golf in, but it's also about feeding yourself with uplifting and helpful information that will fuel the motivation to keep you moving forward in positive steps in your family life.

Action expresses priorities. —MAHATMA GANDHI

Summary
CHAPTER 3: READY TO ROLL: YOUR ROLE WHILE YOUR TEEN IS IN TREATMENT

- Parenting a special needs or struggling teen can be like shooting an arrow at a one-foot target from a great distance. Where some teens would make any parent look like an expert (shooting at a five-foot target), others take a much more skilled and practiced approach.

- While your teen is away, you have the opportunity to make a frank assessment of your own parenting and contributions to the situation. Creating a résumé of failure can help you fairly look at mistakes you have made, and determine the strengths you have gained in the process.

- There is an ideal balance in the program/parent partnership. It is a sweet spot between being micromanaging and laissez-faire. We call it an engaged collaborator.

- Opportunity exists for remodeling your relationship with your son or daughter. Apologizing, asking for forgiveness and creating a vision for your future relationship together is infinitely more valuable than simply warming things up.

Do This Now:
Set aside an hour for writing your résumé of failure. Then follow it up by designing a lofty vision for your future family relationships. This should be captured on paper so you can refer back to it to measure your commitment and progress.

CHAPTER 4

Jeopardy: What's Waiting after Discharge?

"Lower your expectations of earth.
This isn't heaven, so don't expect it to be." —MAX LUCADO

My brother and sister-in-law own a delightful little cabin that they generously allow friends and neighbors to use. At the end of a long winter, they were informed that spring had sprung and their yard was a disaster. They needed to get up there and do some work before it became completely overgrown and beyond redemption. Feeling frustrated, and low on time, they loaded the kids, lawnmowers and weed whackers into a truck and set off for a "fun" Memorial weekend work party.

Upon arriving they were greeted by grass knee deep and a sea of white-headed dandelions. Everyone groaned as they realized the hours of work and weeding that lay ahead. Suddenly, the vivacious five-year-old Eliza squealed, "Look at all those wishes!" (She was referring to the game of making a wish and then blowing the seed "umbrellas" off the stem.) There was a pause, and then Dad started to chuckle. That was all that was needed to break the tension and get everyone laughing, talking and diving into the project.

Expectations

I use this story to illustrate the expectations you may have of how this transition will go and of what your teen will be like when he or she finishes treatment. I'm cautioning you with the reality that you may have to shift those expectations to something more realistic. The adults in the story wanted to see a green, manicured lawn around their cabin, not a field. When their daughter pointed out what a beautiful field they had, they choose to see it through a new lens and acknowledged the beauty therein. Get ready to acknowledge the good and real growth in your son or daughter. You may not get everything you wanted, but you can find great satisfaction and joy in seeing *some* of what you hoped for.

Up to this point, my suggestions and stories have been upbeat and hopeful. Now I need to switch gears a little and talk to those of you who are in denial about how critical and truly difficult the transition will be. I am a glass-half-full kind of person myself, but it is my mission and duty in writing this book to leave you educated and prepared. I don't want to see you left devastated when the first challenge arrives. No matter how many times I forewarn you, when something happens, you are still going to feel your world rock. I beg you to remember the phrase, "Hello, resistance (or threats, or anxiety) … I've been expecting you." Do not put down the book or skip ahead. Face your fears, and realize that you have already managed some of the most difficult parts of the process. Now you will need to finish strong. I've witnessed hundreds of successful outcomes over the years, and I know it can be done. With your experience, your love for this teen and the steps in this book, you can do this.

Greenhouse to Garden

As you have learned, programs are designed to be highly structured environments in which a lot of nurturing takes place. Everything inside the walls of that program, or that particular "world," is designed to encourage growth and nurture improvements along the way. A greenhouse serves much the same function as a program; it's a place for seeds to sprout, reaching for the sunlight, forcing roots into the nutrient rich earth, protected in a climate-controlled environment, and safe from crowding, weeds or other destructive forces that would stunt their growth. The gardeners are routinely feeding, watering, checking for disease and bracing the tender stalks of the plants. Some are even playing beautiful music to encourage health in the plants. Sounds like a nice job, doesn't it?

Eventually, however, the greenhouse will turn the plant over to a part-time, novice gardener, who will take the plant out into the real world in order for it to reach its full potential. Transplanted into a natural setting, the young plant will experience a challenging transition. Even if the greenhouse staff sends the part-time gardener on her way with detailed instructions, invitations to call with questions and bags full of plant food, she cannot control the environment or conditions outside. If replanted too early in the season, an early spring storm could sweep through and wipe it out, not to mention more mundane challenges like birds, dogs, under-watering or over-feeding.

The natural environment of your home and family has far more variables than the garden, not to mention that your teen's development, because of personal choice and individual differences, is far less predictable than that of a plant. Then there are the "weeds": bad friends, drugs/alcohol, technology, academic stressors and a myriad of other destructive elements that the program has protected them from. These are the oppositional forces that work against the growth that has been so carefully nurtured inside your teen. And unlike the program staff, who are replaced every few hours by a completely fresh staff, you can't realistically devote all your time to the care and monitoring of your teen.

After all that has been invested, it makes sense to gain knowledge, build a plan and have support in the vital process of transition. And while the last ten years have seen a tremendous increase in the level of parent education offered by most good programs, too often much of that great preparation flies out the window when the teen comes home and old patterns—and problems—begin to take hold again. My job and my vision has been to educate programs, professionals and parents on how to prepare families and their teens for the hidden waterfalls they will encounter downstream after discharge and help them manage it with a plan and the confidence to side-step the challenges if possible. The rest of this chapter will introduce you to those challenges through stories of families we have worked with.

Pack Early

One mother, who still had six months before her daughter's discharge, called to get our help. When I commended her for her foresight, she told me she liked to pack her suitcase early for her journeys. "It takes the anxiety out of the trip," she said. Knowing that she was prepared and had what she needed in her suitcase brought her peace. Again, she was calling me months in advance, rather than scrambling to pull things together two to three weeks before.

I appreciated her foresight and it's paying off for her now. She seems to be following habit number three—Put first things first—that Dr. Stephen Covey talks about in his classic self-help book, *The Seven Habits of Highly Effective People*. He may have been the first to put into a matrix two competing elements that require our time and energy: those activities that are urgent, and the activities that are important. Dwight B. Eisenhower, long before Covey put his matrix in print, summed up the principle nicely with these words: "What is important is seldom urgent and what is urgent is seldom important," and therein lies the rub. Often, things that are important in the long run, but are not urgent at the time, are put off in favor of dealing with things that are "urgent." Yet, if we were to log everything that feels urgent in our lives, we'd discover that in the grand scheme of things, most of them are not important. Placing this transition plan at the center of your focus will allow the plan to be the urgent *and* the important driving force it should be, rather than a harried response to every fire that flares up. This chapter will prompt you to get the suitcase out on the bed, throw open the closets and dressers, and take advantage of the time you have to deliberately pack, considering the climate, the activities and the duration of your adventure.

Hidden Waterfalls

As I go through these following "hidden waterfalls," or jeopardizing situations that you may or may not be aware of on the transitional journey, if you are deliberately self-aware and have done your homework, you will recognize which waterfalls are your own "signature" dangers. Let me suggest here again that your program therapist and your hometown therapist can offer valuable insights as you pack early.

Discordant Parenting Waterfall

The first principle to talk about is discordant parenting; it is mentioned first—as well as in previous chapters—because it ranks in my top two major stumbling blocks for the families I work with. As I've counseled before, you must be able to present a united front, at least on the biggies. There must be a very clear hierarchy and structure in the family, with you, as the parent, at the top. There are several reasons why parents will lose their place at the top. They are seeking peace, so they avoid addressing issues when they arise. They move to being their child's "friend" too quickly in the child's maturation, rather than remaining the parent. One parent has a stronger personality, or that parent's approach is more favored by the children, so collusion with the easier parent begins.

Beth

Beth's mother Patty placed her in a wilderness program. At home in Maine she was cutting, depressed, involved in risky sexual behavior and refusing to abide by the visitation arrangements to see her mother. Her dad, Conrad, was against the placement so Patty came up with the money, went against his wishes, and sent her away for treatment.

Conrad was so angry and upset that he was unwilling to participate in the process that the wilderness program offered. He and Patty had been separated for several years, but they were still slogging through all the ugliness of wrapping up the divorce. The divorce was finalized while Beth was away at the program.

Fortunately, Conrad's heart softened as he received weekly letters from Beth and saw her steady and promising growth. Near the end of treatment he decided to go out and visit her in the wilderness. That ended up being a turning point for him; when he saw the maturity and confidence in Beth's face and speech, it brought him around to realizing that maybe his ex-wife wasn't such a bad person after all. Maybe it had been a good thing, especially given the fact that he hadn't paid a dime. He had maintained a firm denial up until that point that Beth needed any help, and definitely not something as extreme as wilderness. Because of his come-around in the woods, when Patty suggested having aftercare support from the program staff, he was open to the idea.

When I made my home visit to the family, Patty walked into the house behind me. Anxiety was high but manageable because I had helped both agree to manage their emotions, put their animosity for one another behind them, and follow my lead. Over the next two days, we sat in his living room and hammered out a consistent approach to their parenting, so that when Beth was at Dad's house, she lived by the same rules she did at Patty's. Before this, Conrad had been the weak link and had allowed Beth to literally run wild. Patty, to balance that, had taken on the role of strict enforcer with curfews, homework, and so forth. When Beth returned from treatment, she tested them big time, trying to break up this newly formed treaty. Eventually her attempts to break it up lessened as she saw each parent committed to communicating, backing each other up, and maintaining their leadership role and expectations of her.

Things went extremely well for several months. When I followed up some time later, I was expecting great news. Unfortunately, Dad had backslid, rationalizing and excusing Beth's defiance of the rules he and Patty had agreed upon in his living room. This was a green light for Beth to run headlong through the gap in their expectations of her. She hooked up with some bad friends and stopped seeing her mother altogether. She moved in with Dad permanently because he was the obvious path of least resistance. Nearly all of the progress she'd made in treatment was lost. Conrad had toppled over the waterfall of wanting so much to be Beth's friend rather than her parent that he had undermined both the home contract and Patty in the process. It may be easy, but it is rarely smart, to do what comes naturally when change is what's really required.

> It may be easy, but it is rarely smart, to do what comes naturally when change is what's really required.

Emotional Trigger Waterfall

Whenever we ask parents who are calling us for assistance for a brief history of what led to their teen's treatment, it is never brief. It is a loaded and emotionally laden request. Before treatment, families experience trauma around a troubled teen's issues. All the events they've been through that created such emotional upheaval prompt a stress reaction to certain words, smells or actions of their teen.

While your son or daughter is away, you develop more hope and optimism because you are shielded from the day-to-day interactions with this child. You feel that you are growing, changing and forgiving quite well. However, these traumas are so deep, when your teen comes home, little things will be said or done that remind you of the old days. Even if it's extremely mild, the experience can trigger powerful emotions, with fear being one of the biggest.

One mother, whose daughter was in the treatment program, visited her during parent days. By all accounts, this girl was doing quite well in the program. Despite Mom's very best efforts, she was emotionally triggered when her daughter rolled her eyes and huffed, "Whatever ... Have it your way." It reminded Mom of the "old," pretreatment daughter and before they knew it their communication had exploded into a full-blown argument. Later, on the phone with me, she expressed the hopelessness she felt at that point because she said, "That happened in the treatment program. We weren't even home alone and I fell into this."

The combination of the history, the emotion and the fact that you care so much makes you vulnerable to triggers like this. Triggers can be as small as a drooping head with downcast eyes that make you mentally jump all the way to a possible suicide. Or it could be the mention of a certain friend's name that has you picturing a drive to the local jail to bail them out. Or perhaps it's a request for help that has you feeling overwhelmed by the thought of being a caretaker for the rest of your life.

Some common triggers are:

- Rolling the eyes

- Name calling

- Wanting to see a certain friend

- Refusal to do something

- Taking something without asking

- Rudeness

Did you feel your blood pressure rise just reading that list? When there is a history of trauma between parent and child, most parents experience what I call PPTSD, or Parental Post Traumatic Stress Disorder. Unfortunately, when the parents are triggered is when the biggest relapses occur with the teenager too.

Holly

One family that illustrates this experience perfectly is that of Holly and her parents. They were doing well on many fronts. Mom and Dad were maintaining boundaries and had set expectations of their daughter. There were certain friends with whom she could not hang out, and also certain kinds of social events she could not attend. Before treatment, she had been involved in drugs, drinking and hooking up with some really bad characters.

Holly came home one Monday after school and mentioned in passing a party to be held that weekend. The parents did a great job of saying, "I'm sorry. You can't go. It's not going to be a good environment for you." She continued to ask throughout the week and became increasingly angry that she was not allowed to go to the party. She insisted that some good kids would be going too. However, the parents found out through some of Holly's peers that the party was the same kind of event that had caused problems in the past.

Holly became increasingly belligerent, refusing to do things, yelling at her mom, calling her names and swearing. Finally, her mother lost her cool and slapped her daughter across the face. Mom had done phenomenally well all week with this issue until the moment when she snapped. Holly left home on her own accord and went to the party without permission. There she had her first drink of alcohol after treatment and proceeded to get drunk. It took a lot of work on everyone's part to rein this whole situation in again. What Holly admitted at the end of her time working with us was very revealing: "You know, I wasn't going to go to that party. I was just mad at my parents for not letting me go, so I took it out on my mom, but when she slapped me, that gave me permission to go."

I don't want to suggest that all of the pressure to make this work is on the parents. I'm just trying to highlight what a huge role you have in this, for good or ill. Understanding what could potentially be a trigger for you helps you brace yourself emotionally and watch for it. The next test will become your moment to shine.

Power Struggle Waterfall
Sophie

One morning Cathy's 16-year-old daughter, Sophie, did not get up for school. When Cathy asked why she was still in bed a mere ten minutes before the school bell would ring, Sophie replied she wasn't going because only a half-day of school was scheduled that day. Instead of reminding her of the consequences, as agreed upon in the family rules, Cathy became angry and took away the outfit she had bought Sophie the day before. Sophie growled and pulled the covers over her head. Five minutes later, Cathy returned and told Sophie she would be grounded for the weekend if she didn't get up immediately.

Sophie refused and just lay there. Not knowing what else to do and now being full engaged in the power struggle, Cathy threatened to not let her daughter go to the National Dance Conference that was coming up in a few weeks if she didn't get up and go to school immediately. Sophie became even more upset and defiant.

The easiest thing in the world for parents to do is to get involved in an escalating power struggle. This waterfall relates closely to triggers and, because education was this family's trigger, Sophie's refusal to attend school brought back all kinds of intense memories and fears of relapse for Cathy who overreacted. If this story sounds familiar and

Trigger Turnaround Exercise

Take a minute or two to list some of the first triggers you will likely experience when your teen comes home. Now list them for the co-parent as well, because they are very often different. Keep in mind that some of these triggers may be coming from your co-parent.

Then, beside each trigger, label the emotion (anger, shock, helplessness, fear, bitterness, etc.) that accompanies the trigger and rate it's intensity on a scale of 1−10.

Next, watch where your thoughts go and identify your exaggerated belief (e.g., they didn't change at all; they're going to end up in jail; they obviously hate me, etc.).

Finally, determine what a more rational belief or thought would be. (e.g., this is an old habit they are still trying to break; this is a bump in the road and I have a plan to handle it; their anxiety is getting the best of both of us and we need a break.)

To download a template of this table visit **www.NotbyChance.com**

power struggles have been a theme in the past for you, you should realize that you will need to manage your emotions and put in place a concrete "next step" to avoid them in the future.

Freedoms/Privileges Waterfall

Picture the Grand Canyon-sized divide that exists between the structure in the program, and the structure you are able to maintain at home. If you don't create a ramp, there could be a free fall off the edge when a teen is given too much freedom too soon.

Jocelyn

Jocelyn's parents wanted desperately to provide her with the opportunities necessary to take initiative in her life. They didn't want to hold her accountable for her household chores, because they were afraid that doing so wouldn't allow Jocelyn to make her own choices. They reasoned that if she didn't make good choices, "We'll just talk to her." Now, as transition coaches for the family, we warned them about having clear expectations and consistent accountability. If they didn't maintain those standards, they would be prone to frustration and likely to slip into power struggles, possibly fostering the same manipulative dynamics that existed before Jocelyn went away for treatment. But they wanted to try it their way first.

Jocelyn didn't show any inkling of the initiative they wanted her to display. Consequently, her dad blew up, taking everything away from her at once, which he regretted and backed down on an hour later. Jocelyn continued her old noncontributing ways and Dad felt like a failure. He came back to us, wanting us to help them start over. Imagine how much harder it was to begin holding Jocelyn accountable for her chores at that point, rather than on the first day home, when all kinds of changes were being revealed. The golden opportunity of using the transition from treatment to home as a springboard for new behaviors had been lost.

Rory

One wonderful family in the Midwest worked doggedly to set up a maintainable set of family rules and consequences. Unfortunately, as their son Rory's attitude began to slip, they looked to granting the use of a cell phone as a way to throw him a bone, and build a more friendly relationship. Although their coach had encouraged them not to give his cell phone back right away, Rory's parents did so. To those of us on the outside, it was obvious that not only had Rory's parents sent him the unmistakable message that they wouldn't follow through with the expectations they had established with him, his program therapist and our coach, but the return of his cell phone had predictably in his case, tempted Rory to reconnect with his old negative buddies. Though Rory had been sober for almost two years in treatment, having a cell phone was too much freedom for him to handle right away, and he relapsed back into drugs and alcohol. His parents corrected their mistake with the phone right away, but it took many months before they could correct the course Rory was on.

Both Jocelyn's and Rory's parents needed to trust the process and the power that consistency, structure and timing provide. What a boost it would have been to their own leadership role, their confidence and their teen's long-term success if they had managed to successfully handle the Grand Canyon of difference between the program and the home environment. Though they don't often want them, most teens need authority figures and rules in their lives to help make some of their decisions *for* them until they're mature enough to do it for themselves. By losing sight of the standards you set, by making excuses or self-serving rationalizations, or by letting yourself get worn down by badgering, you're risking all that you and your teen have worked so hard to accomplish. I know this takes incredible stamina, but remember that you have already invested 75 percent, and this last 25 percent is the most important part of the contribution. Don't assume that all teens coming from treatment can't handle a cell phone. That's not the point I'm trying to make. Recognize instead, that these parents didn't stay true to the plan that was customized for their specific situations, and they were swept right over the waterfall.

Not Knowing When or How to Let Go Waterfall
Calvin

Calvin needed to move out when he came home to Oregon; he was over eighteen and both parents felt the time had arrived for him to become more responsible. They set him up with an apartment and told him he needed to get a job. He didn't and would call every month to demand money for rent and food. He played on their fears by saying things such as, "You don't want me to be homeless, do you?" It worked every time; they'd cave in and send him the cash.

Mom and Dad had set no clear intermediate boundaries. They continued to pay for Calvin's cell phone in case he got into trouble and needed to call them—even though he wouldn't answer when they tried to reach him. They didn't know how he was spending the money they'd given him, but he continued to get it. He was not progressing, and they felt more and more as if they were being held hostage, with no answers or end in sight. Calvin would play video games all day and then tell them he was depressed and couldn't get a job because no one would hire him. Everyone involved felt helpless and stuck.

Calvin's transition home was further complicated by the fact that he was also on the threshold of adulthood. The transition to independent living is always tricky, even when teens aren't struggling or in treatment. We will be covering the launch from the nest in greater depth in Chapter 13.

Over-accommodation Waterfall

Sometimes in their desire to find solutions, parents become too accommodating.

Corinne

We worked with Florida parents who were struggling with their 13-year-old daughter, Corinne. She would get started in one school, have problems, and demand that she be sent to another school. She would give her parents a very convincing and tearful speech on why it was impossible for her to continue at that school. The parents, who were divorced, ended up moving her to three new schools in one year.

Unfortunately, they weren't aware that while they had great intentions, they were actually doing much more harm than good. They were reinforcing Corinne's belief that they would rescue her if she just claimed she was incapable and overwhelmed. By over-accommodating her unreasonable demands, they were letting her dodge responsibility and stunting the growth she would have experienced had they insisted she stay where she was and work through the social and academic issues. For parents of teens with disabilities, this waterfall could be your biggest danger. Remember to prepare the child for the path, not the path for the child.

Unclear Expectations/No Accountability Waterfall

As parents, we are programmed to want to see our kids succeed, but often we are so anxious to see it happen that we lower the bar to a level that they can too easily sail over.

Graham

One family from New York came to us because they had tried to take their son Graham from a treatment program straight into college without support. Unfortunately, everything was set up for him without much effort or input on his part: apartment, roommate, class schedule, and so on. He also lacked a clear understanding of the expectations and the consequences of not doing the work. The fact is that if teens are not willing to help do the work to apply to college, they tend to not work once they are there either. Sure enough, after only one month, Graham called his parents begging for a plane ticket home and even threatened to hurt himself if they didn't do as he told them. Out of fear, they complied with his request and brought him home, again without setting any expectations of him. It was no surprise that they found themselves right back in the same situation of feeling powerless and helpless.

Can you imagine your teen coping with a treatment program that does not set clear expectations for students' behavior? The teens would be adrift; the program would have no way of holding them accountable, no way of helping them to advance through the process, and chaos would ensue. Accountability can only be created through first setting clear expectations—and we'll put pen to paper on that topic in Chapter 7.

The Social Vacuum Waterfall

Another waterfall that is probably one of the most visible of them all is what we call the social vacuum. A lack of positive friends and mentors is a real problem for kids coming out of therapeutic programs. Humans have a fundamental need for friends and when a teen comes home after months or even years away in a treatment program, everyone is understandably anxious about that teen's lack of social relationships at home. Social vacuums are eventually filled, but unfortunately, a vacuum tends to pick up the dirt. Less desirable friends invariably seem to be the most available to fill this social vacuum.

Landon

Landon came home to Arizona from a short-term treatment program. One of his big issues was attracting unsavory friends and girlfriends. His parents had gone through a process of identifying friends whom they would be willing to let him associate with, as well as those former friends whom he was not allowed to see. He had pretty much agreed to meet those expectations, while the program therapist and our transition coach were guiding him. But that was before he got home. Literally, the day after he returned home, one of his friends, who wasn't necessarily the worst friend on the list, but certainly wasn't the best, called and wanted to see him. The parents understood what this social vacuum meant for Landon; they knew it would to be filled by somebody and Landon had been doing a pretty good job of "kind of" complying with some of the family rules. So against their better judgment, and our guidance, they agreed to let Landon's friend visit their son. They justified their actions with the thought that they wouldn't let Landon leave home with his friend.

(You can see how this can turn into a slippery slope.) The boy came over and he and Landon reconnected.

It wasn't long before Landon said, "Hey Mom, we are just going to run to the 7-11." Not wanting to look unreasonable or have conflict in front of Landon's friend, his parents said "You can stay out for two hours, but you need to be home for dinner by six."

By doing this they were violating the very parameters they'd worked so hard to set. Predictably, their plan backfired; Landon went out with his friend and ended up not rolling in until about 10:30 that night. The parents were relieved that the kids hadn't been drinking or misbehaving in any other way, so they compounded their mistake by making another big one: not following through with the consequences they'd laid out ahead of time. After that, there was no way to bring Landon around to the transition plan again. Within a couple of weeks he was hanging out with the very worst kids in that little community, and that's when his parents completely lost control.

In Chapter 6 we will talk about the value of having a home team, one of the most important uses of which is to fill the social vacuum. In reality, teens genuinely want to be successful when they get home; they really do. When they first come out of the program, they're looking at their lives from a loftier perspective, and they are appreciative of their families and all they've been given. Often they write letters to the parents or talk to them over the phone and express their dreams of the day they can be home and rebuilding their relationships with their families. Naturally, parents hold those letters and conversations close to their hearts, and as I said, the teens really, truly mean what they say, most of the time.

But teens are extremely naïve when it comes to the wisdom required to avoid relapse. They have not yet been through the process of having to dramatically change their lives and then go back into the real world and have their resolve tested. I would say that 100 percent of the time they are caught off guard by how forceful the pull of those friends, some temptations, and the complexity of the real world can be.

Julia

During her treatment program, Julia had written wonderful letters to her parents in South Carolina, saying all the things they wanted to hear: how she'd changed, how much she loved them and wanted to spend time with them, and how she was looking forward to leading a better, healthier life away from destructive influences. Based on these letters, and against the recommendations of her professionals, Mom and Dad decided to bring her home rather than send her to a residential program for further treatment.

Within hours of being in her old environment and knowing her friends were blocks away, she started requesting time with them. That triggered her dad's anger. He growled at her, "We were manipulated. You were lying to us. You just want to be with your friends and you had no intentions of spending time with us." This was the beginning of a rapid downward slide for the family; distrust started to take over on both sides. Julia retorted, "You haven't changed either. You're just like you were before too." Without a plan for the friend question, everyone was sucked into the pull of this dangerous waterfall.

Siblings Waterfall

One of your greatest tools for loving and fortifying your teen may be a brother or sister. But in some cases siblings can also be the instigators of a downward spiral.

Travis

Travis was from New Mexico and finished a year in residential treatment after completing drug rehab. His older brother welcomed him home with a little private celebration, showing him how he could use spice instead of marijuana to get high, right under the noses of their parents. Later the older brother admitted it and said he felt it was okay and wanted to give Travis a way to get high without getting caught. The parents let this older brother stay in the home even though he was over 20 years of age and still using drugs. The brother ended up ushering him back to a lifestyle the parents had spent tens of thousands of dollars trying to close the door on.

Sometimes jealous siblings will actively undermine a teen's return home. Things were nice while the troubled teen was away. The house was quieter and less stressful. Now they have to make room for them in the use of the car, use of the computer, getting their bedroom back, and especially in sharing Mom and Dad's attention and time. Resentment can surface in different ways: through a cold shoulder, squabbling or by direct accusations—"She didn't change at all! Look at what she's doing"—getting Mom and Dad to focus on all of the negatives rather than shining a spotlight on the positives. Many times, these siblings have been ridiculed or tormented by the troubled sibling, so even though they may love their sibling as a brother or sister, they sure don't like or want that sibling around. This can lead to some sticky family dynamics that may require professional intervention to solve, but in any case it's clearly something to discuss prior to the return home. Believe me, siblings are watching the countdown to reunion, just as you are, but with a lot less control.

Do you see how crucial the first few days and weeks at home are? Do you see why these metaphorical hidden waterfalls can be upon us before we know they are coming if we aren't prepared with a game plan? Transitions are rarely smooth. There is no such thing as perfection when human emotions and other people are involved. However, in the next few chapters I will help you map the river so you can move through the phases of transition following treatment with as little fear and as few plunges as possible. River trips can be fun if you are prepared and have a guide. Let's take the ride together.

Summary
CHAPTER 4: JEOPARDY: WHAT'S WAITING AFTER DISCHARGE?

- Expectations must be managed, or we will overlook the real positive changes in our teen while focusing on the negative irritants.

- In comparing the transition from treatment to home to that of a plant going from the greenhouse to the garden, there are environmental challenges that must be compensated if a tender plant—or teen—is to thrive.

- Remember to focus on activities that are important, not just urgent. Knowing the difference will keep you from stamping out fires only to sacrifice activities or changes that would have had the most positive long-term effect.

- As you study the "hidden waterfalls" included in this chapter, you will recognize which waterfalls are your own "signature" dangers. Your program or hometown therapist can offer valuable insights here.

....

What to Do Now
Complete the Trigger Turnaround Exercise found at www.Not-byChance.com. Have your co-parent also complete the exercise and compare and discuss your personal revelations. Awareness is half the battle.

CHAPTER 5

Stack the Deck: Your Community's Contribution

"You can always tell a real friend; when you've made a fool of yourself, he doesn't feel you've done a permanent job." —LAURENCE J. PETER

The ex-convict was returning home by bus after many years away. He turned to his seatmate and confided that he was a paroled convict returning from a distant prison. His imprisonment had brought shame to his family and they had neither visited nor written to him very often. He hoped, however, that it was because they were too poor to travel and uneducated to write. He hoped that they had forgiven him.

To ease their embarrassment, he asked that they tie a yellow ribbon around the old oak tree on their farm, which was near the road he would come into town on. This would be the signal that they had forgiven him and wanted him home with them. If they didn't, the tree would be empty and he would travel on through.

As the train neared his hometown, the suspense became so great he couldn't bear to look out the window. He begged his travel companion to change seats with him and look for the tree himself. The minutes stretched for what seemed like an eternity. The companion finally broke the silence by saying, "You'd better take a look, Son." When the young man squinted out the window, to his amazement and relief there were not just one, but one hundred yellow ribbons tied to the old oak tree.

Whether you can hum the tune to the hit song, "Tie a Yellow Ribbon 'Round the Old Oak Tree," or not, you would have to be

pretty hard-hearted not to be moved by this story. If a loved one has been away, serving in the military, or for whatever reason, a yellow ribbon is a beautiful symbol of love, acceptance and forgiveness. I retell this story—not to label your teen as an ex-convict or anything of the sort—but to remind you that coming home again is a critical

moment in your teen's story. You want to make this as welcoming, loving, motivational and set up for success as possible.

Community is Key

In the last chapter we mentioned the idea of getting friends and neighbors involved in the process of supporting your teen's return from treatment. Let's talk about why this is so crucial, and how to go about making it happen.

You may think of your teen's time away as strictly family business. Why does community matter, especially your community? It matters because that's where young people who are growing up inside that community start to develop a sense of themselves, and a sense of self-esteem driven by the idea that other people besides just their immediate family care about them. Sure, Mom and Dad love you; they have to. But if other people care about you, watch out for you, and go out of their way to talk to you and encourage you in your life, that means an awful lot.

Remember my idea of using video cameras in our work? I want to assure you that not all of my ideas were so bright but ineffectual. Now I'm going to tell you about another idea that was there from the inception of Homeward Bound, probably because I'd seen it work firsthand. This fundamental building block is worth its weight in gold, and the idea is one of the game changers for adolescents at risk, both before treatment and certainly after. What I'm talking about is fostering one or more natural mentors for your teen.

Natural vs. Assigned Mentors

Evidence of the benefits of natural mentors (e.g., neighbors, teachers, relatives, coaches, etc.), or relationships that are organically formed, has been shown in recent studies and is also born out in my professional experience. A natural mentor, on the whole, is far more effective than an officially assigned mentor. Why is this the case? Let's step back and talk about how therapy works and then compare it to mentoring.

There have been many studies that have tried to determine which therapeutic model is more effective, and what it boils down to is that all of them are essentially equal in their effectiveness. But it is the "common factors" that produce the lion's share of any successful outcome in therapy. From Michael Lambert's 1992 review of the outcome research, we know that one of the greatest common factors in therapy outcome is the relationship between the therapist and the client.

Mentoring is based on the same principle. The relationship between the mentor and the mentee is one of the keys to whether that relationship can produce positive change. The other key is the longevity of the relationship. It may be a good relationship, but if it ends prematurely—doesn't last more than a few months—it will not have any influence on a teen who is going through years of ups and downs in adolescence. This is where the difference between natural mentoring, provided by individuals within the teen's social network, and mentoring by someone assigned by an outside agency, becomes obvious.

Formal mentoring relationships in which the mentor/mentee relationship is both close and sustained are very difficult to achieve. In fact, studies suggest that most formal mentoring relationships last less than a year. In contrast, natural mentoring relationships, which come from the church, school, family and neighborhood are far more durable, with average relationships lasting almost nine years (e.g., DuBois and Silverthorne, 2005; Zimmerman et al., 2005). Other studies have also shown that formal mentoring programs tend to achieve relatively small positive effects (e.g., DuBois et al., 2002 and 2011).

Let me illustrate the power of this principle with an example from my own family. One of our sons went through a period where he struggled with self-esteem. He was quiet, depressed, and anxious. We didn't know how to reach him, and any encouragement to try new things or call a friend was met with a "I hate that," or "I don't like them." Finally, we decided to reach out to our community and ask for their support. We told them briefly about some of the things we were concerned about and asked them to share their insights, and just to be aware. We weren't asking them to take him to lunch, but if they could see some way to encourage him or include him, we would have really appreciated their stepping forward to do so.

The support and concern started rolling in immediately. We received e-mails from his teachers that assured us he was a happy and helpful kid in class, and they offered to keep an eye on him. Others offered to take him to a *Star Wars* movie when it came out, knowing he was a mega fan. One uncle asked him to teach his two young sons some karate moves so they wouldn't get beaten up any more. We had older boys who were black belts, but this uncle didn't ask them. He chose instead to make our struggling son the expert and mentor. You should have seen him light up. Not only did it build his confidence in himself, but it built everyone else's confidence in him as he rose to the occasion.

After a few years of maturation, and the many spontaneous and creative contributions of others, we have been amazed at his courage, his gifts and his determination. We still have days when we worry, as we have with each of our children, but not as we used to because now we have observed and tracked his progress and know he will have the skills, self-esteem and support to thrive.

The challenge families have today is that the concept of community—of being in an area where you're close to extended family and the people around you know you well—seems like a relic from some far-off good old days, like a Norman Rockwell illustration of a family dinner scene. Today, it's not uncommon for extended family to be scattered from Washington to Florida. We're constantly uprooting ourselves and moving to follow career changes, making stability and continuity even harder to come by. Many of us are also uncomfortable about sharing our problems with others, whether it's because we're ashamed of our struggles, or because we don't want to trouble other people.

You may have good reason for feeling embarrassed by your teen's history of misadventures in the neighborhood or school; you may feel like pulling back, closing the door, drawing the blinds and trying to deal with your child's issues on your own. Part of that is fear that other parents don't want your child around theirs, because they're afraid for their own children—and their concern may be legitimate. The unfortunate consequence of this is that all too often we wall ourselves off from the very people who could be our greatest allies, and we turn more and more to professionals for that help instead. I'm not against using professionals—after all, I'm one myself—but the result of our society becoming less community oriented is that our kids don't get the benefit of the thousand micro-interventions that they need during adolescence as they make weightier choices and define who they are.

Talking About Treatment

When it comes to parents being open about sending a child to a treatment program, we've seen the whole gamut of behaviors. We've seen some families comfortable with being extremely open and sharing worries or good news with their inner circle and the people they love to build support for their teenager. But we've also seen parents who literally wait until summer to send their kids away to a short-term program so that they can tell their friends and neighbors that their child is away at Grandma's, or church camp, or whatever sounds most believable.

There are five big problems with this approach.

1. You aren't really fooling most people, as they've seen trouble brewing, in some cases for years.

2. You undermine their ability to step up and be a part of the solution. In effect you're saying, "We don't talk about our daughter or son being in treatment, and therefore you shouldn't ask about it."

3. It teaches your children to lie, and that this situation is something to be ashamed of.

4. There is no one to celebrate wins with during treatment or later, when your teen returns home.

5. Remaining superficial hijacks the opportunity to create deeper relationships, and serve as a support to others in their own personal and family struggles.

I advise you not to promise your teen that you won't tell other people where they are. What you can promise is to be selective and sensitive to who knows. You don't have to, and shouldn't, shout it to the world through a mass e-mail or Facebook post, but you can delicately share the information with the right people. The reality is people are honored to be included in your inner circle and will go out of their way to mentor your teen once he or she comes home. The home team can be one of your greatest strategic advantages as a mom or dad, and in the next chapter we'll talk about all the ways you can maximize its effectiveness.

You can't hide a teenager. People notice when teens stop coming and going, aren't at the family celebration, or the cell phone stops texting back. Below are my suggestions. I hope you take them seriously as they are born from a decade of watching these stories unfold. You need to be ready with a positive and truthful answer for the inevitable questions.

Acquaintances

How do you answer queries from people you will run into at the store or while picking up the mail. They aren't your closest friends or family. They don't need to hear it blow by blow; they just need to know that your teen has been struggling with life and is away for a while getting some help. That's about all they need to know and you have not shared anything too personal. The truthful but vague answer will let them know to not ask too many more questions.

Make sure you do not lie. It may be tempting, but it's wrong, and second, it's a huge weight to bear as a family. When siblings are taught the story they must tell, they have to keep up the charade, which is an uncomfortable and unfair burden to place on them. It will come back to haunt you when your son or daughter comes home and has to continue the lie, which will make that child feel ashamed of being in a treatment program. Secrets and shame don't allow for repentance, restitution, forgiveness or celebration of growth.

"For every good reason there is to lie, there is a better reason to tell the truth." —Bo Bennet

Siblings

There is so much to say about siblings and especially younger siblings who are still at home and have had to witness all of the fighting, tears and late night calls. Their involvement with the struggling teen could range from alignment to neglect to actual abuse. They too desperately need your leadership and attention throughout treatment because they are dealing with a whole host of emotions themselves:

- Anger

- Fear

- Relief

- Shame

- Resentment

This is all normal and understandable. If your teen is already in the treatment program, you have probably had to navigate some of these waters with your other children on your own. But if you are still attempting to work through this, here are some suggestions:

1. Bring them into the inner circle of your confidence. Tell them what you have been shielding them from, in an age-appropriate way.

2. Let them express their feelings to you and especially to their sibling through letters, as directed by your program therapist.

3. Get them professional help too if they are severely traumatized by what's happened.

4. Assure them that you sent their sibling away to get help, not because you were angry. You also can assure them that you don't plan on sending them to a program as well.

5. Allow them to express their feelings. It may take them a while to come around to seeing things as you do. Be patient, for they need time to process the idea of the necessity of the separation, just as you did.

Extended Family and Close Friends

Whether you are fortunate enough to live close to grandparents, aunts and uncles, or if they are across the country or world from you, they can still provide you with a great built-in support network. They may need to be educated about the process or brought up to speed on what's happening, but they shouldn't be ignored. In all my years as a therapist, I have rarely seen a truly crazy family, though many of my clients have tried to claim that title for their own. Just as with your other children, these relatives need time to adjust to the idea of treatment.

If you encounter shock, blame and strong opposition, do not let it derail you. They have not been there for the late night hunts for teenage parties, or the melt-downs at school, or the police intervention. What you have done may sound extreme to them, but that's what the situation called for. If you are patient and take the time—and it will take time—to tell your family's story, most people will understand why you felt it was necessary. Some may never understand, and it's okay to distance yourself from them for a time, especially if their attitudes and messages are toxic. You need to surround yourself with people who can support you and your teen, not side with them against you and the treatment process.

You've seen the intervention reality shows on television. A person bent on self-destruction with drugs or other dangerous behaviors is brought into a room where people who are significant in that person's life are waiting to share their love and explain what that person's behavior is doing to their relationships. Interventionists will do this because a crystal clear, united voice must break through the denial that's obscuring the struggling person's vision. By letting your family members in on the process, they can become active contributors to its success. Their letters of compassion and encouragement and commitment to the process will be gold to your teen in those months away from home and especially when your teen returns home.

Plan these conversations earlier rather than later. This not only goes for your children, family, close friends and acquaintances but for the school administrator, your clergy member, team coaches and others in the loop. Keep it upbeat so that they can be prepared and willing to help during the transition home. You'll be amazed at how accepting and understanding people can be. Family and close friends can be a powerful influence even from miles and miles away. They can lift where they stand, but only if you direct them where to lift, or in other words, exactly how they can help. Invite your program therapist to suggest what family and friends should write in letters to benefit your teen. Should it be a letter of encouragement, or a message of hope, or a message that others are imperfect too so your teen should not give up? Or should that letter contain a "step-it-up" message from your teen's favorite uncle or grandparent who can get away with giving a "kick in the pants" through a loving but challenging letter?

If you do run into criticism or judgment, just remember that this comes with the territory when people are ignorant of the issues you've faced as a family. I've had many parents tell me that their extended family and friends were "shocked" to hear that their teen was in a "boot camp." However, in time, most of them will fully support the decision and even want to step in and be a part of your teen's life when that young person comes home.

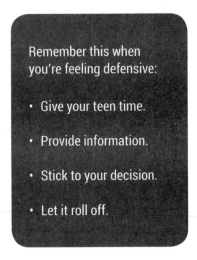

Remember this when you're feeling defensive:

- Give your teen time.

- Provide information.

- Stick to your decision.

- Let it roll off.

Later, when we talk about creating your *home team*, you will see that the support and influence of key adults and peers can create magic and motivation that a parent simply can't duplicate. At Homeward Bound we've created an online tool for families called Family Bridge, which is used to keep family, friends and professionals connected with the teen throughout the treatment journey. It is much more impactful when everyone gets up-to-date information, sees pictures, reads letters and is investing continually along the way. They can also send messages of encouragement and pictures back to the teen.

Amelia

Amelia's father was downright excellent at asking others to join in the change. His daughter had alienated her positive friends and their parents, and was on thin ice with neighbors and school officials. Her father reached out to everyone. Though initially worried about not having enough positive peers, he eventually came up with three. The program that she was in did not use Family Bridge, so he became the hub of information, staying in touch with the program and making sure pictures and letters and good news were shared frequently. Home team members responded and sent their own pictures and encouraging letters back to Amelia. Her father must have had 50 people involved. Amelia was flooded with mail, which not only made her feel extremely loved but proved that her home team was proud of her efforts and honored to be involved in her journey. Eventually, when it was time for her to come home, these relationships were warm and current. There was no awkward avoidance of the subject; it was a wonderfully smooth social transition.

Get Connected with Other Parents

As I mentioned before in the parent/program partnership, whether it's through parent days, parent conference calls or local support groups, I strongly encourage you to get to know some of the other parents in the program. They could be among the most rewarding relationships you have because there is no one on the planet who understands your situation better than the other parents. I know some parents who want to attend the workshops almost as much to see the other parents as to see their own child. They require that validation to continue the fight.

Kim Buczkowski, a former Homeward Bound parent, said, "The 'brotherhood of the broken hearted' is a powerful thing. After years of being judged by well-meaning family and friends, we finally found true understanding by those who had walked the same road we had. It also helps to know your story isn't one of a kind. Over and over you hear pieces of what you've been through spoken by others. It is somehow soothing to your broken heart … to realize you aren't as terrible a parent as you've been beating yourself up to believe. Finding others with children who are experiencing so many things like you are, due to issues like addiction, depression, Asperger's, ODD, ADHD, etc., helps you understand it's not all your fault; you didn't do it *all* wrong (although we learn what we have been doing wrong). It frees you up from beating yourself to exhaustion, and allows you to keep moving forward."

Micro-interventions

I didn't think so at the time, but I was fortunate to grow up in a very small community where everyone knew the Thaynes and therefore knew me. The sense of community was strong and ever present. I remember one incident in particular: As 11-year-old boys will sometimes do when they are bored, my friend Jeff, my brother Tracy and I came up with an idea that would land us all in big trouble.

We lived just a short bike ride away from the only highway that traversed the rural countryside; leading into a gorge we called the "river bottom." As we stood at the top of the hill one day, one of us said, "I bet you can't throw a dirt clod down and hit that yellow line on the road." Well, hurling clods of dirt quickly commenced and the fun began. It was easy to judge who was winning, because as each clod landed, a small dust cloud would rise and leave a brown dirt mark on the black road. When the first car approached the gorge, we stopped throwing, not wanting to hit the car, but then we had our next "bright idea"; what if we lobbed clods just a few feet in front of the cars? We would of course land them far enough ahead not to hit the car. I remember saying something like, "Seeing the dust will wake the driver up, maybe startle them a little, but we won't do any damage." (Can you see where this is going?)

Unfortunately, one of us threw a little late and hit a passing windshield. Fortunately, no accident followed, but the driver hit the brakes and before we knew what was going on, the car was in reverse, quickly coming back up the hill after us. We scattered to hide. It couldn't have been more than 60 seconds later when the red, angry face of a man who lived in our community appeared. He knew me by sight and what's more, he knew my parents.

After telling me that I had broken his windshield, he said, "I know your dad and mom and I know they didn't raise you this way. You had better go home and tell them what happened before I do." With the sting of his words ringing in our ears, we raced home to face the consequences, and consequences we received.

This experience ended up providing a significant intervention in my life, one of literally thousands of what I now call micro-interventions, most of which were warm salutations, good-natured teasing, smiles and genuine praise for any noteworthy accomplishment. I often wonder what kind of person I would have become if I had not been daily surrounded by others who knew and cared about my family and me. They corrected, encouraged and loved me. Sometimes their mere presence was enough to keep me in check. I have no doubt that these micro-interventions had a massive, cumulative effect. I knew I belonged, and that my decisions mattered and affected not only me but many others around me. There would be disappointment or celebration depending on my choices. I was not an island. I belonged and was valued. The more I see of families who are isolated in their efforts to raise their teens today, reaching out only to professionals for support, or struggling through on their own, the luckier I feel about my childhood and adolescence. Small towns may have a bad reputation for gossip, but they gossip mostly because they care. I'll take that any day over a community that doesn't care.

Community Building in Our Day

Now, before you pound a *For Sale* sign into your front lawn, and head out for the next small town you can find, let me assure you that it's really not necessary. I'm not raising my own family in that exact situation—though I continually hint at it to my wife. Building such a network of support around our families is more important than ever, but it doesn't happen spontaneously. It takes going outside comfort zones, finding people we can trust to share our experiences with. A lot of parents feel threatened by what they see as the cut-throat social competition that their young people are swimming in—who's the best athlete, who's going to an Ivy League school—which gives them yet another reason to hide their problems and their kids from view.

But in my experience as a father and as a therapist, I've found there's something deep inside most of us that causes us to want to help. It's a natural part of being human.

Recently I read a story of a heroic act, where a random group of bystanders, construction workers and college students near Utah State University joined together to lift a burning car off a motorcyclist who was trapped underneath. The inspiring event was captured in a moving 60-second video that went viral on YouTube. When I did the Google search to find the story, I typed in "channel 2 news burning car." Lo and behold, another story popped up of a man in Georgia who, a week earlier, had risked his life to save another stranger in a burning car! The story went on to say that this man had unsuccessfully tried to save his own sister from a fire many years earlier. You could feel the pain behind his words when he said, "I tried. But today, I feel good because I did what I … I didn't get to fulfill in 1956." What a long time to have to wait! In both events, the rescuers were called heroes and angels. They were in the right place at the right time, and they possessed the right instincts.

The media inundates us with stories of violence and crime, portraying a world in which altruism seems to be extinct. But in reality, most people are good. Most of us would respond to help a person in crisis, especially when someone takes the lead and shows us how. We are privileged to tap into the hero network every day in the in-home work we do. Our families are the beneficiaries of people simply doing what comes naturally, stepping in where help is needed, offering whatever they have available to offer. These heroes don't have to charge through flames to be given that title. Most go quietly about their day until the moment when the opportunity presents itself to step up and save someone, literally or figuratively. (Watch for my next book, an inspiring compilation of these natural mentor success stories.)

Summary
CHAPTER 5: STACK THE DECK:
YOUR COMMUNITY'S CONTRIBUTION

- Coming home is a critical moment in your teen's story. You want to make it as welcoming, loving and motivational as possible.

- Research indicates that natural mentor/mentee relationships have a greater chance for success than a formalized mentoring relationship. Based on proximity and longevity, a natural mentor relationship lasts an average of nine years.

- Be honest about your son or daughter being in treatment. You can share enough information for people to understand that intervention was necessary, without scaring them off or ruining your child's chance at acceptance and forgiveness when they return.

- A caring community environment for a young person will produce thousands of spontaneous micro-interventions on that young person's life path.

What to Do Now
Make a mental list of the people who have had a positive effect on your life. Though you may never have labeled them as natural mentors, recognize now their influence on you through spontaneous words of encouragement or shared experiences.

CHAPTER 6

The Cheering Section: Recruiting Multiple Natural Mentors

"Alone we can do so little; together we can do so much." —HELEN KELLER

Drew was a great surfer at 17, having spent every moment possible on the California beaches near his home. His family was well loved in the coastal town where his father had been raised. After Drew finished a residential treatment program, he returned home. His parents were more than willing to reach out and created a large and committed home team. After we all gathered in their back yard one evening where Drew spoke of his journey through treatment, each of these people was given the green light to reach out and help. There were multiple ways and times over the days and months that followed when his parents did indeed reach out and use those teammates to keep Drew progressing.

One example of how this happened involved their next-door neighbor. Drew was prone to becoming enraged, threatening and physically violent. Instead of his parents immediately calling the cops, they called the next-door neighbor—whom Drew respected. This man knew why he had been asked to come over and was happy to do it. This action immediately de-escalated the tension by introducing someone new into a system that was in crisis, changing the dynamics completely. The parents felt calmer, knowing they had some back-up and they were able to respond with cooler heads. Drew toned down what he was saying and how he was saying it, not wanting to disappoint this friend. Before, the only tool in Mom and Dad's toolbox was to resort to calling the cops if he didn't calm down. By this point such a strategy had lost any real effect on Drew.

He also had a schoolteacher whom he loved and who truly cared for him in return. She was invited to be on the team and she was happy to accept. As part of his transition plan, Drew had become involved in a big-brother type of organization, where he would help the kids with special needs and then play basketball with them afterward. One day Drew wanted to quit, so Dad texted the teacher to let her know and ask if she would find a way to encourage him to stick with it and continue going to practice. She did so. Because of her neutral demeanor and her positive track record with Drew, he didn't feel a need to resist her and agreed to stay on the team. Though these instances seem small, they were both critical decision points that kept the discipline and use of new communication skills learned in treatment rolling. This one was among my Top 10 Stellar Home Teams. You don't need to expect your home team to match it, but do allow it to inspire your thinking and planning.

Identifying Home Team Members

You may be wracking your brain looking for potential teammates, and coming up with nothing. Why is this? Susan Maushart suggests, "Our, quote-unquote, family rooms are docking stations now. We have five hundred or six hundred *friends* and no idea who our next door neighbors are. We affiliate with 'communities' based on trivia—a mutual appreciation of bacon, a shared distaste for slow walkers. We have sold out social depth for social breadth and interactive quality for interactive quantity to become what playwright Richard Foreman calls 'pancake people: spread wide and thin as we connect with that vast network of information accessed by the mere touch of a button.'" (Maushart, 2010). So in our day and time it might be more difficult, but it is far from impossible. Even parents who swear up and down they have no one to ask, surprise us time and again with wonderful mentors who seemingly come out of the woodwork.

Who's a potential recruit for your teen's home team? They can be the obvious professionals like teachers and therapists, but I want you to broaden your perspective of who can be sup-

> Research shows that the more powerful mentors are generally those who are already in the teen's inner circle, or who can be brought into the circle based on shared interests and proximity.

portive to include people we like to refer to as natural mentors, such as coaches, religious leaders, coworkers, extended family, parents of other teens, neighbors, family and friends. These people are in natural positions to provide mentorship. They can rescue, guide, counsel, teach, listen, help in skill development or just love and enjoy time with your teen or with you. Sometimes families struggle to find good mentors, so they hire them. This can be helpful and we promote this as an option, but remember from the last chapter the research shows that the more powerful mentors are generally those who are already in the teen's inner circle, or who can be brought into the circle based on shared interests and proximity.

It has been so important to have a team ... to create the village. It wouldn't have occurred to me to celebrate my daughter's homecoming, I was gritting my teeth I was so nervous about everything. But that summer some of her friends would call her and tell her they wanted to include her in something; they wanted to support her goals. However, there would be drinking. It was hard on her, but those friends wouldn't have treated her in that kind and gentle way if they hadn't come to our home for our celebration and learned what their responsibilities were as good friends. —PARENT (MONTANA)

As you brainstorm to find people you can bring into the home team, you should keep in mind at least three general areas of support they might offer. Think about each of the three types below and identify who you know who would be a good fit for each one.

1. Companionship: Those who provide companionship are able to enjoy time with the teen or the parent simply for the sake of having a good time. They share meals, stories or mutually enjoyable activities together.

2. Emotional Support: Those who give emotional support are those who are able to listen, show acceptance and affirm the work or the person, appropriately offering thoughts and directions.

3. Instrumental Support: Those who can provide instrumental support will give concrete assistance, teach new skills or provide opportunities and material resources. Here we're talking about both natural mentors and professionals, and in fact, most teens coming out of treatment programs will still benefit from having an outpatient therapist or being involved in group counseling once they've come home. I would encourage you to plug into a support group in your community, either in person or online. As you share your experiences with one another, a bond of friendship forms and the members of that community support group become a part of your natural support network. Generally, parents whose teens have already gone through the treatment process appreciate the value of professionals and see the probable need for continuing therapeutic or medical support, which is why I'm focusing mainly on the idea of natural mentors.

What should we look for in mentors? Go to www.NotbyChance. com for a simple brainstorming exercise to help identify individuals and their strengths and resources applicable to reinforcing your fragile teen—for example, they own a local grocery store that often hires teens; they coached water polo all the time they were raising their own children; they have a daughter who will be attending the same school as your teen this year, and so on.

Extended Family

Family members—grandparents, aunts and uncles—have a long history with your teenager and an extended future with them as well. These folks are sometimes the very best supporters for a returning teen. They know from years of experience and observation your teen's strengths—as well as yours—better than most. They have a vested interest in the success of your teen and their involvement springs from a place of true caring. That sincerity is not lost on teens, who are expert on reading the difference between those who are there for them because they're expected to be, and those who are there for them because they choose to be. Oftentimes grandparents—despite how quirky you think they've become in their old age—are admired and loved by their grandchildren.

Older Siblings

Other typical members of a home team, whom I've often seen play a positive role, are older siblings, be they full, half or even step siblings. Older brothers or sisters can make stellar mentors. Many times, growing up, the teen has looked up to this sibling and even followed in his or her footsteps, for good or ill. The reality is that an older sibling probably enjoys being looked up to, loves the younger teen, and will behave better than he or she normally does. An older sibling who loves a younger brother or sister can't bear the idea of relapse. Take this opportunity to invite the very best behavior and leadership from your older children. Educate them on the teen's social and medical history and the treatment journey, and point out the specific ways you see them reaching out to listen, cheer on and set an example. Invite them to commit to a high standard of conduct for the good of the team, letting them know they may be the ones with the greatest chance for making a difference.

Toby

Toby's older sister, Kate, was his idol. Unfortunately, she had also been a horrible influence on him when they were younger. She was the one who initially introduced him to marijuana and got him smoking with her. She had subsequently left home and gone down the wrong path for a while herself. However, around the time Toby was coming out of treatment, she asked her parents if she could move back in. This was a huge dilemma for them because they wanted her kind of influence as far away from Toby as possible. Still, at the same time, Toby's dad felt that although he had kicked his daughter out of the home, maybe this would be his one opportunity to heal that relationship.

Mom and Dad met with me to talk about this transition and whether Kate should come back into the home. They decided to let me meet Kate. I found her to be a very loving older sister, and at a place in her life where she was beginning to make positive changes. She had stopped using drugs, gotten a job and desperately wanted to make amends by providing a good role model for Toby. Now I wouldn't recommend this in every situation, but in this instance it made a lot of sense to bring the family back together and to manage two transitions at once. That ended up being a key relationship for Toby, who quickly realized that Kate was more of a third parent than a party buddy. It sort of stunned him at first; you could see he was thinking, "Where did my partner in crime go?" But we supported Kate in staying strong and in the end, she really became the hero of the story, thanks to the deep empathy and belief in Toby's power to change that she brought to the table.

Conversely, there are certainly older siblings with whom it would not be in the teen's best interest to encourage contact. In some cases they not only model poor judgment and questionable lifestyles, but may also actively undermine the authority of the parent. So be judicious—but stay open to the potential good that can come from involving older siblings. The mentoring effects can ripple for generations.

Peer Mentors

Another example of important home team members is your son or daughter's positive peers. Unfortunately, a lot of kids who've been away have lost touch with their good friends, and two or three years of real struggle may have passed before they went into treatment. So when they come home, they may have been out of touch with positive friends for quite some time, if they ever had any at all. If at all possible, you may want to reconnect with some of these positive friends. Over the course of time these young people may have grown up and become stronger, more mature and committed to positive lifestyles. With that maturity, they and their parents would be more likely than before to be comfortable with the idea of reconnecting and "being there" for an old friend. When teens still have several months left in treatment, letters provide an especially safe way for parents to allow old friends to reconnect. They can coach and monitor things from a distance. This is one more reason for you to begin thinking about the transition now.

Sterling

Sterling's family invited three of his former friends to be a part of his home team. The big issues for Sterling were his quick temper and tendency to get physically violent. He had gotten into a lot of fights before he was sent away, and his anger frequently got the better of him at home too. His friends were actually very timid kids, which amazed me because Sterling was so outgoing, bold and boisterous. He was obviously their ring leader. I wondered how these guys were going to help him. He'd run them over. But what happened was really an amazing testament to the power of inviting people to be there for the teen in the halls of the school, at the party or on the field when Mom and Dad can't be.

Two weeks after he got home, Sterling went back to school, where he had been doing pretty well overall. But on this particular day, he faced a tremendous test: a kid started to push him around. That was all Sterling needed to come completely unglued. He took this kid down in the hallway and was literally on top of him with his hands around his throat, choking him before anyone realized what was happening. Miraculously, the three friends that I'd met in his home a couple of weeks earlier were there. They looked at each other and quickly confirmed that this was their big moment. These three grabbed him and pulled him off the other boy. Sterling was angry with

> You can't have a therapist following your teen around at school, but you can have people who are invested in your child's success inserted in different arenas of your child's life.

them for intervening, but they stuck with him, held him back and eventually cooled his rage by talking him down. Once he was calm enough to think rationally, they convinced him to walk with them to the office of the assistant principal, who also happened to have been brought into the inner circle of trust. Because she was already "in-the-know" concerning Sterling's challenges and his goals for doing better, she handled the necessary consequences in the very best possible way. Sterling was sent home to take the rest of the day off.

He came back to school the next day and had no more problems for the rest of the year.

Imagine what the likely upshot would have been if the parents hadn't invited the school administration into their family's story of struggle and healing. It could have had a very different outcome, not only for that day but possibly for the rest of Sterling's high-school career and life—yet another powerful testimony of the need for micro-interventions.

You can't have a therapist following your teen around at school, but you can have people who are invested in your child's success inserted in different arenas of your child's life. These key individuals can help shape the future for your teen as they get involved to provide that little bit of buffer, intervention or encouragement needed in the moment. If you catch yourself thinking that you don't have anybody like this that you can call on, remind yourself that we have done this with hundreds of families over the years. I can honestly say that in my experience that is almost never true, because we will serendipitously find support in places we didn't expect. At the end of this chapter, I want you to complete the simple exercise mentioned previously that will help you brainstorm a list of individuals who could play a role in supporting your family or teen in this transition.

Adult Mentors

Another thing to remember is that if you can't find a positive peer, look for an adult mentor, someone who can help your teen in some way. It might be that this person has a hobby in which your teen could take an interest.

Jake

Jake was over the moon about guitars, guitarists and music in general. His parents knew this. They were acquainted with an older gentleman who had a passion for guitars and teaching guitar, so he was one of the first people they introduced their son to when he came home. It was a new relationship, not an existing one, but their common passion for music brought them together and the man became a very consistent and effective mentor to Jake during his weekly lessons.

Madison

Madison returned to her home in Las Vegas following her equine-centered treatment program. When she walked in the door, her parents had an application waiting for her to apply for work at a nearby arena, cleaning out stalls in exchange for horseback riding lessons. The seasoned instructor there became a trusted voice, echoing what Madison's parents were commending or trying to inculcate.

Family History

Maybe you're still shaking your head in disbelief and thinking, "Nice thought, Tim, but you don't know my family, or my town, or this neighborhood. We don't have anyone like that to call on." Let me give you an example that can work for anyone, an inspiration for you as a parent, as well as for your teen, no matter who you are or where you live.

Braveheart

One of the things we like to do in our family is tell stories about individuals in our family history who have overcome trials and tribulations and who, despite challenges, rose to the occasion and showed qualities and strengths that got them through. I personally am convinced that I am a descendant of William Wallace, aka Braveheart. Because we come from the same town in Scotland, and there was so much intermarrying back then, I would bet we have some of his blood in ours. You get my drift? I don't have proof, but I like to tease my kids that Uncle Braveheart would be proud of them.

Even if you have some black sheep or skeletons in those dusty old pictures or written letters, characteristics or stories can always be ferreted out and used for good examples. These are people and concepts that we want our kids to connect and identify with, and that is essentially what you are trying to do with the home team. You are trying to forge relationships with people they look up to. I've shared a lot of stories with my own children about my grandpa Harry, including their favorite story, "Grandpa's Pickax."

Harry

The story began a few years ago when, after months of coaxing, my mother and father finally convinced my grandpa to move in with them. He had been a widower for years, and was mostly wheelchair-bound, due to his knees and hips being "gone." Immediately after relocating, Grandpa's drive to be productive pushed him to look for things he could do to contribute to the family. Each day he would arise early, dress for the day, eat and then "go to work"—and he always found work to do. My parents had long talked of turning part of their ranch into a family park for big family gatherings and reunions. Grandpa caught the vision and decided to take matters into his own hands by clearing the area of sage brush and trimming all the dead branches from the many cedar and pinion pines.

Never asking for help, he found the head of an old rusty pickax. Having learned resourcefulness during the Great Depression, he searched until he found an old, discarded, wooden baseball bat, which he whittled down into a handle with his pocketknife. Then Harry Thayne went to work.

Every day, he drove his motorized wheelchair down the 100 yards of dirt trail from the house and somehow, with a crutch, shovel and pickax, started the process of clearing. While his strength was probably 10 percent of what it once was, "can't" or "too much work" were not in his vocabulary. By the end of the summer he had collected a huge pile of brush and limbs to be burned, and the edge of the pick ax had been polished from use till it shone.

As an excavator, my dad owned all of the equipment to do the job in under an hour. But it wasn't about getting the job done. It was about work, being productive and loving your family enough to serve them each day. What took Grandpa an entire summer could have been accomplished in minutes with a backhoe. But this story would never have been created, nor would the symbol of his legacy. That baseball-bat-handled pickax hangs over our family room fireplace today.

By sharing that story, we highlight the value we place on hard work and resourcefulness. Is there someone in your family tree with a story that illustrates values that are important to you—something that you'd like your teen to understand or cultivate? Is it a story about faith, compassion, genius, good-humor, persistence, adventure or sacrifice? Pull out a picture, if you have one, and tell your teen the story. Let your teen know how he or she is connected to that person—and generously point out the good qualities in that person that you see shining through in them. That person becomes

> **You can make a mentor out of any person whose good qualities reflect the values you believe are important and positive for your teen.**

a mentor, not in body but in spirit. If you've named your teen after an ancestor, talk about that namesake. Your teen will love it. You can make a mentor out of any person whose good qualities reflect the values you believe are important and positive for your teen. Whether it's a living relative, an ancestor, a great leader or some special figure in your faith, the important thing is the sense of connection you create. All of those kinds of stories give your teen a perspective on what's important in life and you the opportunity to point out your child's positive attributes.

Adoption

"But my child is adopted," you may say. Hopefully, you've found ways in the past to help that child feel like a part of your family or "clan." Pride is where you choose to find it. Look at your teen's accomplishments in treatment. It's likely that your teen comes home with new, hard-won skills that his or her peers don't have, whether it's survival skills gained from living in the wild, or rock climbing or the confidence to look someone in the eye. Capturing and labeling those points of pride helps teens see themselves in others, historical or familial, who've overcome obstacles in their own life stories. Use those accomplishments to help your son or daughter see how he or she is tied "in experience" to these strong and positive role models, regardless of the gene pool.

If this home team concept makes you feel uncomfortable, as if you want to crawl into your shell and hide, I want to remind you of something. Humans are social beings. Teenagers are 10 times that social; whether they have a lot of friends or not, they are very attuned to what others think of them and the need to belong is paramount to just about every other aspect of life. If you have given your son or daughter a break from a negative social network by sending him or her to a treatment program, those negative friends could still be lurking around, wanting to become involved in your kid's life when they arrive home. You can help your teen avoid relapsing into those destructive relationships by surrounding him or her with positive peers and mentors. It is a lot harder to get rid of something you *don't* want than it is to fill the space with something you *do* want. That's what the home team does. It fills a social need to be cared for, to belong and to be loved.

Should I Hire or Find a Formal Mentor?

There may be cases in which hiring a mentor is the best option you have. There is no shame in this. In fact, accessing a person with valuable skills and added accountability can come from having a paid or professional mentor. We have mentors on our staff we can bring into the home team. They're friendly, on an upward track themselves, great with teens and young adults, trained in our model and supportive of our mission of maintaining gains made in treatment. If you can't identify the right natural mentors, you can contract outside agencies or clubs to find role models or leaders for your young person. Our kids can't have too many positive mentors in this difficult world we live in.

Though focused mainly on mentoring in the workplace, the book *Power Mentoring* by Ellen Ensher and Susan Murphy suggests some relevant yes or no questions that a teen could answer in evaluating his or her relationship with a mentor. Answering these questions can help your teen realize that a mentor can be found in some unlikely places, and that there are no set prerequisites for a potential mentor.

1. Did I meet my friend through an activity we both enjoy?

2. Did I see someone similar to myself when I began talking to my friend?

3. Did we bond over something similar in our backgrounds?

4. Did our relationship become closer as we did more things together?

5. Did I really feel this person understood me?

6. Did I share some of my fears with this person?

7. Did this person disclose some personal events to me?

8. Did I feel supported by this person when I talked about a problem I was having?

9. Was there a specific event that brought us closer?

10. Was there a specific occurrence that cemented my trust in this person?

Overcoming the Bystander Effect

There's an interesting phenomenon that you need to be warned of. Having multiple mentors, even a group of people invested in your teen, has awesome potential. But beware of the bystander effect, which is a social psychological phenomenon in which people are more likely to help someone in need if they are alone rather than in a group with other people around. Experiments have been conducted that consistently show that the probability of help is inversely related to the number of bystanders.

So how do you reverse the effect and foster group action? First, someone must be the first to move. Altruistic individuals are among those most likely to do so. Now the pressures of conformity have been released and the barrier to helping lowers. The more people who take action, the easier it is for others to do so, especially if they know what they can do. Ambiguity is one of the reasons people hesitate to act. It's good to pull someone out of the crowd and make them a special mentor. A simple approach can be effective: "Hey Belinda, Sarah really looks up to you and I sense that she would listen to you. She's struggling right now with ___, and I'm wondering if you could find the time in the next few days to take her out for a burger and just spend some time together."

Jill

Let me share one more story to drive this point home. I was inspired by Jill, a Texas mother who put her trust in our processes in spite of her discomfort over what I asked her to do. When Jill was told to invite friends, family and any influential others she could think of to her home to celebrate her son, Matt's, graduation from treatment, she swallowed hard and hesitated before saying, "Okaaay …," because she'd been telling people that her son was away at camp, without giving them the real deal. Matt also didn't want to tell anyone where he'd been and why he was there. In fact, he would have loved to bury the whole experience somewhere deep in the backyard if he could have. He certainly didn't want to invite lots of people to his house to celebrate his return from a place he felt embarrassed about. But like most of our teens, he went along with it.

At the appointed hour guests started showing up to the home. They were neighbors, family friends, childhood friends Matt had before getting into trouble, along with their parents, his school principal, their pastor, the school counselor, his band director, a former nanny and extended family members. Jill followed the program in faith, reached out and was overwhelmed with the response. In all there were over 40 people who showed up to hear his story and celebrate his homecoming. Amazing things happened as people reached out to Matt in love and affirmation of the changes they could see in him. He demonstrated confidence as he showed the group what he had made with his own hands while in the wilderness. The director of his private school asked him thoughtful questions and counseled him with wisdom. His band director exuded warmth and a mentoring spirit, excitedly engaging Matt in plans for the upcoming year and ways he could develop his musical talents and passion as a teacher's assistant in the younger grade classes. The mothers of two boys in his class asked me what their sons could do to help.

By the end of the night, the boy who'd sworn to me that he "had no friends" was swimming and laughing with five other boys from the school. The principal was pumping my hand and promising he'd do all he could to help this family. Others were supportive of Jill both for her choice to get her son help and for honoring them by asking for their support. While this is not a "they-lived-happily-ever-after" ending—because the story will continue to unfold for years—the fact is Matt has started to rewrite his story, not only in his mind but in the minds of those who knew him. There will be continual and difficult tasks ahead, but Matt's mentors have captured the momentum of treatment through a planned transition process and a powerful social support network. His mentors are both numerous, passionate and in positions to help him through the tough times.

I honor this mother and all of you readers for being willing to put your trust in us—and in our field in general—to do uncomfortable things for the love and success of your child. You inspire me.

Ready to send out an invitation? Find a sample invite that will give you some of the phrases and wording that can be helpful when you call or write to a potential home team member.

Go to *www.NotbyChance.com*

Summary
CHAPTER 6: THE CHEERING SECTION: CREATING MULTIPLE NATURAL MENTORS

- When brainstorming ideas for potential recruits for your teen's home team, look beyond the professionals such as therapists or teachers, and reach into the pool of natural mentors such as coaches, religious leaders, coworkers, extended family, parents of other teens, neighbors, family and friends.

- Identify which general areas of support each individual might offer: companionship, emotional support or instrumental support.

- Use individuals from your family history, or historical or faith-promoting characters to draw parallels with your teen's positive character traits. Help your teen build his or her identity on the positive similarities you find between those inspiring individuals and your teen.

- Pre-empt the bystander effect by reaching out to invite help before it's needed. Give direction and permission, and home team members will respond in timely and creative ways you haven't dreamed of.

....

What to Do Now
Brainstorm your list of individuals and then go to www.Notby-Chance.com to download the template, How to Ask Someone to Be on Our Home Team. Tweak it to make it your own and relevant to specific recipients and send it out to the list.

CHAPTER 7

Let's Make a Deal:
The Excitement Phase

Those weeks preceding Jay's coming home were wrought will all kinds
of feelings. We were, of course, thrilled and excited that he was coming
home, but there was an enormous amount of anxiety for my wife
and me, wondering was Jay's growth sustainable? Were we prepared
and confident in our own growth to be able to hold the boundaries
that we knew were going to be tested? So I would say it was a very
emotionally volatile time, just because you're so excited but so nervous
as to whether things were going to fall apart. —**Parent, GA**

Your family has been through weeks, months, or possibly years of treatment. Now you are preparing for the graduation and reunion with your teen. You are about to enter transition. The following graph illustrates four phases you can expect to move through as a family.

Four Phases

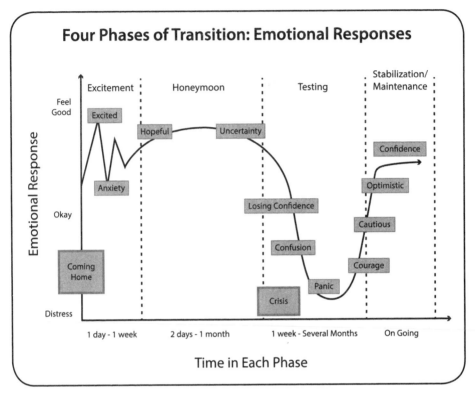

Four Phases of Transition: Emotional Responses

This first phase, which we call the excitement phase, is experienced both by parents at home and by the teen themselves. It begins around the time that your teen starts to realize, "Alright, I'm getting close to being finished here." The prospect of being able to come home to more freedom, family and friends will trigger a lot of emotions in the teen. Of the two major emotions felt during the excitement phase the first, of course, is excitement—but there is another one that's often less obvious, and that's anxiety.

Teens who are close to returning home may feel anxious for a myriad of reasons: fear of messing up and being sent away again; fear of voicing concern about messing up because mentioning that concern to parents might signal that they aren't ready and they will be left in treatment even longer; fear of relapse itself because they want to be successful and happy. They could also fear what old friends and neighbors might think of them, and that they'll be stigmatized for having been put into treatment. Added to these worries is their concern for the future. What lies ahead for them? Will they eventually be able to become independent? Of course, they are also concerned about what kind of privileges they will receive when they get home, and if they are going to have to badger their parents for every little freedom. They are not looking forward to that conflict, though they do want those privileges back.

The anxieties that we see parents experiencing are around some of the same issues: fear that their son or daughter is going to relapse into old, unhealthy or dangerous patterns; fear of how their child will connect socially with other people and find the right friends; fear their teen will fall further behind in academics. Parents also experience anxiety about their own abilities to do their parts well. Looking ahead to the kinds of challenges, or waterfalls, that we discussed in the previous chapters, parents recognize there will be problems and they are fearful about them. So, both parents and teens fluctuate between excitement and anxiety during this phase. In fact, it's fairly normal to see kids take a bit of a downward turn in their treatment progress as they come closer to the end, because of the anxiety they are feeling. So anticipate that and prepare for it. In the next few pages I will give you suggestions and counsel for each phase, starting with eight suggestions for the excitement phase.

Every tomorrow has two handles. We can take hold of it with the handle of anxiety or the handle of faith. —HENRY WARD BEECHER

Talk it Out

If you haven't done so already, make sure you have someone with whom you can talk about your emotions. Find a therapist or coach who has worked with parents who have been through the trauma that led to treatment and are bringing their teens home again. That counselor will be better equipped to help you through this transition. Nothing will surprise them, not your fears, not your questions, not your situation. Find someone who has a real parenting model for this specific situation and who can train and coach you on how to apply the model.

Besides an expert coach, you can add a trusted friend to vent to. Sometimes hearing your thoughts and feelings put into words and receiving validation or direction from someone you love and trust is the best medicine. You have already identified some great individuals in your home team. Rely on them.

Don't Make Promises You Can't Keep

Sometimes parents feel so excited about their child coming home and so happy that their relationship is mending that they are tempted to hug their child and assure him or her of things that they shouldn't at this juncture. I've seen too many parents promise the big carrot: that the teen will never have to go to another treatment program. And why is that a problem? Because if you take that off the table, you may be giving up leverage that you will need down the line, and that's potentially a huge problem. Think about it. If your teen falls into drug addiction or starts exhibiting such risky behavior that his or her own or another's safety could be in jeopardy, you certainly should leave returning to treatment as an option. It may be the only way to get your child's life back on track. What you *can* say is, "If you're successful, obviously you're never going to have to go back again—but if not, we have to be able to call on that kind of resource if needed."

Don't Cave In to Pressure

Don't allow your teen to pressure you into promising the return of certain privileges. Because teens who are coming out of treatment are experiencing both anxiety about, and the desire to get back, freedoms, they talk to their parents about those issues long before they come home. They want to know what they're going to be able to do, and how soon. They want the return of the freedoms they used to have—for example, cell phone and car use, sleepovers, computer time, dating, time with friends, and so forth. Parents, if there is ever a time to not buckle under pressure from your teen, it's now, while they are still in the program. Now is the time to let your teen be angry if he or she is going to be angry, and let the program deal with the fallout. Let your teen cope with that disappointment, that frustration. Treatment programs are there to help in dealing with disappointments and downturns and frustrations. The more your teen can master disappointment in mature healthy ways before leaving the treatment program, the better.

While I'm asking you not to give in to certain things, it's important to make sure you aren't overly strict about rules you're not planning to follow through on. For example, if you're saying that your teen can't have the cell phone back right away do not bring it with you to the airport. The joy and gratitude you will feel when your child is discharged may pose a temptation to give that phone back too soon. Don't make a rule you aren't willing to back up. Consistency is key. (I want you to go back and underline or highlight those last two sentences.)

Appraise the Friends

Our parents tell us time and again that one of the most helpful exercises we had them complete during the excitement phase was creating an ABC list of friends. Parents work together at home and the teen works with the program therapist on the list at least a couple of weeks before discharge. The time to do it is when there has been a break or a cooling-off period in the relationships and greater perspective has been gained from the vantage point of treatment. You simply list friends based on their qualities:

A	B	C
John	Rebecca	Scott
Sarah	Josh	Lauren
Amy		Tom
		Julie
		Karen

- A-List Friends: These are the friends who were or could be a positive influence on your son or daughter. They may have been dumped or passed over for the last few months or years as your teen was struggling, but they are kids you would be pleased to see your kid strike up a friendship with again.

- C-List Friends: These are the friends that are absolutely off the list. Their further association with your teen is not even to be considered, because of their negative influence on him or her.

- B-List Friends: These are basically those who are left over after completing the A and C lists. You may not know enough about these individuals to be able to rate them, so you will have to wait and see. They may or may not be good examples themselves, but they have the redeeming quality of not having it as their mission to drag others down with them. On occasion you can find a difference maker in this group to whom you can appeal to support your goals as a parent, because they truly care for your child. Proceed with caution, but don't count everyone on the B list out.

You will then need to compare your son or daughter's list to your own. It may not match up perfectly, but you'll be amazed at how honest and insightful your child can be about his or her social life when coming from such a good place. Rarely will someone on your C list of worst offenders pop up on your teen's A (for Angel) list. Take the time to discuss each person you both put on the B list. Really listen to your teen's thoughts and feelings. Get curious and be open to what is shared and then let your teen know you would like to contact these friends to get to know them and give them a chance. Once you have done all of this, you will both be in agreement in most instances, and what a relief it is to have it in writing! When the phone rings or the mention of a certain person comes up for the first time, you've already visited the topic, so you know if you can say, "You bet! Bring them over," or "Sorry, Son. They aren't on the list."

Recognize Progress

By now, you've probably seen or heard about a lot of the growth in your teen, and the excitement phase is a great time to recognize that progress and those new-found strengths. When you see those strengths come out—and you will, in multiple ways both subtle and obvious—make sure you compliment your teen on them. "Hey, thanks for telling me where you were going without me asking." Or "I didn't know you knew how to make breakfast, wow!" A hint of warning here: make sure that you don't overdo it. There's no need to celebrate every little dinky thing your child does right, but be sure you're being very specific about the changes you're seeing displayed. Express your appreciation of the fact that your teen has had to apply himself or herself and work hard to develop those strengths. Share your genuine confidence that your teen can continue developing those strengths when it's time to come home again.

Identify Fears and Prepare

During the excitement phase you need to face any lingering fears you have about bringing your teen home so that you can deliberately plan for what you can do to help prevent those fears from coming true. Chapter 4 was all about helping you look ahead at the waterfalls so you could make early, concrete plans for how to deal with them. If you foster the attitude that these challenges are your opportunity to test-drive your new coping or parenting skills, you're going to do fine. You will have a plan to navigate each waterfall. If you haven't already scoped out the most likely problems you will face and created a plan for dealing with them, now is definitely the time to do it. If you haven't mentally rehearsed your plan over and over again, just having the plan won't be enough. Use this time available to you in the excitement phase to make the plan, rehearse the plan, get help implementing it, and to create a back-up plan.

Dump the Guilt

Let go of any remaining guilt you might have about sending your son or daughter into treatment before he or she comes home. So often you aren't even aware that you are holding this guilt. What that residual emotion causes you to do is to overindulge your teen. I see parents wanting to reward the teen for getting through the program, and they do so in inappropriate ways, trying to make up for the fact that they "sent them away." I've seen parents buy iPhones to present as a graduation gift, or take them to a restaurant and let them order everything on the menu—no boundaries whatsoever. That is common after a wilderness program, because teens have been fantasizing about food and what their first meal is going to be like when they come out of the field after all of the camp food. I've also seen parents splurge and give their teen full spa treatments at a hotel on the way home.

The problem is that by doing all of these things, you're sending the message to your teen that you feel guilty you sent him or her away. What your teen hears is, "I'm not sure I did the right thing, and I regret that I did it." That underlying admission of guilt is a surefire way to undermine both your teen's recovery and your authority.

Nick

Nick's parents started to second-guess their decision to send him away to treatment. He was extremely manipulative and wrote letters about the staff and what was going on, which were not 100 percent true. One of the comments was, "This academic program they have is worthless; it's no good. I am falling behind in school because you sent me to this program. I'm going to be behind my friends in my own grade and I'm not going to be able to succeed or graduate on time now." As you can imagine, this really hit a nerve with his parents. Their confidence in their decision diminished and their guilt grew each time they thought about his statement. They were already lamenting to themselves, "Oh no, he was really vulnerable in school already and now we've set him back even further."

When they picked Nick up at the program campus, he made a point to reinforce that guilt again: "Now I've got to go back into school and I'm even further behind and there is no way I can ever catch up." Instead of dealing with that concern and their guilt with their professionals or in private with one another, they let slip, "We do regret that this puts you back academically, but there were a lot of good things that happened while you were there too." That expression of regret was the only opening Nick needed to seize that nugget of guilt and run with it. Pretty soon he had his parents feeling so guilty about his placement that the entire story of his experience in treatment shifted from, "I really gained a lot" to "I am nervous about going to school, and now I'm behind. So this was an abusive situation. I am going to fail in school because of it." It's amazing how, by expressing that little bit of uncertainty, Nick's parents opened the door for him to manipulate them and completely change the story their family would forever tell of the experience.

So, while it's important that you celebrate your child's homecoming, don't let guilt sweep you away into celebrating in inappropriate ways. As a way to gauge whether your plans are appropriate, remind yourself that you wouldn't dream of serving alcohol at a party celebrating somebody's sobriety, for example. In the same way, it's likely that giving kids unlimited computer time is not the right way to celebrate their return if they'd been addicted to the computer before they left. Allowing them free rein with the car and negative peers will be a disaster in the making as well. While it may sound ridiculous on paper, we do run into parents who feel guilty that they've kept their teens away from their friends for all of those months in treatment. They will then allow their teens too much unsupervised time around kids they don't really know, and relapse happens. Never let guilt be your motivating emotion for parenting decisions.

> **Never let guilt be your motivating emotion for parenting decisions.**

Let me throw in a strong warning here as well, based on my own experiences as a teen, as a dad, and as a professional. Without going into the statistics of teens getting into trouble for the first time, sleepovers shouldn't be considered for at least a few months. They should be reserved for highly mature kids, not someone who recently returned from a highly structured environment where there were few freedoms. Your son or daughter needs to develop a strong and sturdy identity as someone who knows where he or she is going before you turn him or her loose to participate in an all-nighter. Remember, parents sleep. Teens in a group don't. Group IQ decreases with every person you add to an unsupervised group and goes down further the later the hour. Feel free to blame it on me when your teen pitches a fit.

The bottom line about the excitement phase is that it's important to make clear exactly what your expectations are of your teen's behavior when or before your teen comes home. Use the time available to you during the excitement phase to clarify this with your teen. Remember—you, as parents, are at the top of the hierarchy and should be guiding this process, not letting the teen come home and start calling the shots. That doesn't mean that the teen shouldn't be part of the discussion and allowed to give his or her perspective on the issues, but in the end, Mom and Dad, together, take in the information and make the final decision. Showing this example of leadership and parental unity will send the message to your teen that you have changed and that life will be different after the home coming. Keep it positive, upbeat, and collaborative in terms of the issues you can reasonably let go of. Everyone has made changes; everyone has worked hard; and everyone is going to benefit from the growth and understanding gained. You want to prep your teen with, "Hey, we know we were part of the problem in the first place, so we've made a lot of changes at home too." Be specific about what those changes are and how they are going to positively affect all your lives and the environment you live in.

Set Absolutes (Red Light Issues)
We have found that house rules need to include some absolutes, or what we call red light issues. These are rules that, as parents, you must

simply insist on, and the excitement phase is the time to establish what those non-negotiables will be. Keep it to three or four red light issues, but be clear about the positive and negative consequences of those particular expectations. Some issues will be considered yellow light issues. They are situations in which a teen can make some decisions of his or her own—in consultation with Mom and Dad. Lastly, the green light issues involve decisions that a teen can make for himself or herself. As your teen moves to a more mature and independent state, you want to shift toward green light issues, and have fewer and fewer red light issues.

In treatment, with the support of the program therapist, make sure to spell out specifics on computer time, cell phones, drug use, friends, going out, education, chores, and respectful behavior. Pick the issues that were a concern prior to treatment or worry you now in the transition. Don't make a red light issue out of something that's never been a concern.

Five Keys to Fair Consequences

The following are guidelines that will help you set effective consequences:

1. *Discuss the consequences as a family:* Children should have some input into setting up the rules and, ideally, should be given an opportunity to help define the consequences for

breaking those rules. Parents should make sure the rules are appropriate and the consequences are adequate.

2. *Match the intensity of the behavior:* For minor incidents, the consequences should be minor; for major ones the consequences should be more significant. Kicking the teen out of the house for a curfew violation does not match the intensity of the teen's actions. Restricting his or her next night out does match the intensity of the behavior.

3. *Be natural and/or logical:* Consequences should be clearly understood on the front end, and should fit the nature of the behavior. These are logical consequences (e.g., missing curfew might result in being grounded the next weekend evening, and stealing might require the teen to make restitution equivalent to, or somewhat higher, than the value of the item stolen.) Parents should also allow the natural consequences of the teen's actions to occur. Natural consequences are events that occur without parental intervention (e.g., missing school might result in school detention, and skipping a shift at work might result in being fired). If parents allow these consequences to occur, the teen can learn valuable lessons.

4. *Specific amount of time:* Punishments for negative behaviors should be carried out within a specific time frame that is consistent and realistic. Sometimes when parents feel frustrated and helpless, they impose punishments that last "until I say it's over!" Doing this causes the teen to feel hopeless and distrusting. It makes emotional self-regulation more difficult.

5. *Realistic and practicable.* As tempting as it is, parents should never tell their teen that they are grounded "until their eighteenth birthday," or impose any other punishment that is unrealistic or unlikely to occur. When you do that, your teen recognizes that you will not follow through with the punishment, which invites your child to act out even more.

To sum things up, express your relief and joy over the prospect of having your son or daughter home with you again, but at the same time, make it clear that home is going to be different in a good way: the structure and boundaries are in place to create a gradual ramp down from the treatment program to an improved home life.

Summary
CHAPTER 7: LET'S MAKE A DEAL: THE EXCITEMENT PHASE

- Teens and parents both feel the mixture of two emotions during this first phase of transition: excitement and anxiety. These are normal and can be used to incentivize you to do the work necessary before discharge.

- Be ready for the pressure to hand over certain privileges. Do not cave in to guilt or repeated requests if your therapist warns you to proceed with caution.

- Friends are either a great support or a great danger to a returning teen. Use the time before discharge to decide with your teen which friends will support the changes and growth from treatment, and which should be avoided.

- Use this phase to establish absolutes in your home rules on such things as drug use, computer or cell phone privileges, curfews, and so forth.

....

What to Do Now

Create your list of red, yellow, and green light issues. Find a printable template at www.NotbyChance.com.

CHAPTER 8

Stars in Our Eyes:
The Honeymoon Phase

"The greatest happiness of life is the conviction that we are loved; loved for ourselves, or rather, loved in spite of ourselves." —VICTOR HUGO

Looking for a working definition of a honeymoon, I came across a quote most of us can appreciate:

"...the three month maximum period between a person's entry into a new situation and a person's complete screwing up of said situation or essential elements of it. This phenomenon is backed by massive amounts of studies and social psychology and even more massive amounts of personal testimony from bitter, angry people." –UrbanDictionary.com.

You may ask if the honeymoon phase is real, and it certainly is. The definition above is more than a little sarcastic, but it's true in that people become angry or feel duped when the honeymoon goes away. The honeymoon phase is just as real as the other phases of transition that come after it. Appreciate and enjoy every minute of it while it's underway.

How does this phase play out with teens who have been through the excitement phase while still in the program? They've been picked up at the program location or the airport and their parents are enjoying watching their relief at being home. They are sleeping in their own bed. They're eating Mom's cooking. They're enjoying some much-missed privacy, more freedom and less structure than they had in the program; it's a time when many teens feel grateful and happy. In turn, when you have your child back in your arms, you feel the same gratitude and joy to be united again. In most cases your child's sullen or defiant manner has melted away. Your child is now smiling, talkative, expressing joy over the familiarity of home. It is a magical and joyous time, full of hope and pride and determination.

Marshall came home a whole different kid; he was reachable again. He was engaged, he was clear-headed, he was clean, he was sober, and he was warm, fuzzy and affectionate, all those things because he missed us obviously, and because he had time to think. He also came home with lots of new skills and exciting stories to tell. —PARENT (TENNESSEE)

Short, Sweet and Real

Teens' behavior mirrors their appreciation and can sometimes lure you into a false sense of security. Obviously, like all phases, this too shall pass. After all, how many of us who have been married more than a year or two would say that we are still in the honeymoon phase? Not many. It may be a good relationship but not necessarily a honeymoon relationship. It's not realistic to expect to live our whole lives in a honeymoon phase. But just because we are past it, it doesn't mean that our love for our spouse or the other person is not real; it's absolutely real. It's just that we can't ignore the fact that the shine wears off a little. We eventually get into the routine of regular life and have to deal with the socks on the floor, the bills, and the in-laws.

My wife and I recently experienced this with our son returning from his freshman year at college. The first night was all smiles, hugs, stories of funny roommates, and appreciation for the pets, the good advice he'd taken from us and the taste of home-cooked food after a year of questionable cafeteria fare. My wife and I sat next to each other and each of us pressed our leg against the other's leg, under the table, our secret "can-you-believe-this" signal. We basked in a moment of amazement and pride at the growth and maturity he was displaying. We were so content to have him home and looked forward to some quality time together with this emerging adult.

Within 20 seconds of our standing up to clear the table, he announced his plans to borrow the car so he could pick up so and so and go visit so and so who had just got back in town. When we asked for his help with the dishes first, he begged a younger sibling to do his share with a promise to return the favor later. He then leaped over his laundry hamper, which was sitting where he had dropped it in the kitchen when he arrived and, with a shout of "Love ya," he was out the door. I saw my wife's eyes narrow and a growl start to rumble in her throat. It was a short honeymoon, basically one meal in length.

Obviously, teens don't turn into perfectly rational and sensitive adults while they are in treatment, so the honeymoon is not going to last. In many cases your teen has made great strides and you will be thrilled with the differences you see. But teens are not perfect, and expecting them to be so would neither be fair nor realistic.

To finish the story of our son, a month or two after his arrival home, my wife was reading her personal journal of the summer after her high school graduation. She admitted to me later that she blushed over and over as she read. It was disappointingly shallow and could be summed up in the repetition of one word "me, me, me, me, me!" She was dismayed at how it seemed to cycle between what she was wearing, who had asked her to dance, what social event she was going to next, how she had been treated, and so forth. She acknowledged that she sounded just like our son! With that revelation, coming in the form of her own teenage voice from the past, she had a much better understanding of the fact that maturity comes with time, but it does eventually come.

Enjoy It but Don't Falsely Prolong It

I have some suggestions for you in this honeymoon phase. First of all, enjoy it while it lasts but don't try to prolong it by giving your son or daughter what he or she wants all the time, letting misbehavior slide. This is doubly tempting, because we love the feeling of being in the honeymoon phase and we really hate the pain of falling out of it and into the testing phase that's coming next. We have to work extremely hard, as parents, to keep from bending over backward to ensure we keep the soft glow and romantic music of the honeymoon alive.

See Strengths

As I mentioned when I discussed the excitement phase, continue to focus on your teen's strengths. There is going to be a lot that you can compliment him or her on during this time, and it's key to consistently affirm you teen's growth. Make sure you express a lot of appreciation, even if it didn't come naturally to you before your teen left home. A clumsy display of appreciation is better than no appreciation. I'll bet if you commit to this action, looking for contrasts with your child's pretreatment behavior, you will easily find something every single day to praise. Again, don't overdo it by lowering the bar or sounding insincere. This suggestion is meant to help you consciously change your thought patterns so you are attuned to seeing the positives. It was quite easy before to focus on the negatives. Now, I want you to become a talent scout, searching for those emerging qualities in your teen that help you appreciate your child's unique character traits, improved maturity, and growing potential. Focus on those glimmers of maturity and take mental, if not actual, notes. This is not only so you can remember to compliment your teen later but also to remind you that progress has absolutely been made. Here are a few examples:

- A compliment your teen voluntarily gives to a family member

- A towel hung up after a shower

- An astute insight your teen express about himself or herself or the family

- A mature handling of disappointment

Use Momentum

Another suggestion is to use the momentum that's happening during this honeymoon to establish goals and plans for moving forward. Just because your teen is home doesn't mean that all is finished. This is why I like to come out and work with families in their homes during the early stages of the transition. There is more openness and wise thinking, along with more optimism for the future. It's a great time to firm up plans and structure life.

Inevitably, you're going to worry about giving your teen some of the freedoms that he or she is asking for. The Honeymoon is a good opportunity to watch and see how well your child handles that freedom. It shouldn't be big steps; the return of freedoms needs to be gradual, one small thing at a time. But the little things that you're allowing your child to do or have provide that opportunity for your child to prove that he or she can handle them well and is mature enough for them. Don't give your teen more freedom than he or she is ready for, or you will regret it. It's important for you to remember that it is infinitely easier to give a freedom, than it is to take one back. Be wise in doling out freedoms or privileges as your teen exhibits his or her new maturity but be sure to provide opportunities to prove that your faith was warranted.

> It is infinitely easier to give a freedom, than it is to take one back.

Give Up Suspicion

Sometimes both parents aren't on board during the honeymoon phase. One mother told me that when her son came home, she was really nervous, looking for anything to go wrong, while her husband was much more able to embrace the idea that their son had really changed. Please, for both your own sake and for your teen's, put that reflexive suspicion and worry aside, at least for now. This is a time to enjoy what your teen has accomplished and to let him or her see that appreciation. By doing so you're helping to build the bridges you'll need to cross as you travel into the less idyllic phase, the testing phase.

Summary
CHAPTER 8: STARS IN OUR EYES: THE HONEYMOON PHASE

- This is a real and sweet phase. Enjoy it but don't try to falsely prolong it.

- See the strengths in your son or daughter by becoming a" talent scout." Remind yourself of your child's unique and loveable gifts and growth as the honeymoon starts to fade.

- Use the good feelings and lofty thinking to firm up plans and structure for your child's life now that he or she is home.

- Warm up the relationship as much as you can in this phase. There will be bumps ahead, and you will want this connection and warmth to sustain you both.

....

What to Do Now

Visualize these phases so that nothing surprises you. What will tell you that you are in the honeymoon phase, and what will tell you that it is beginning to fade?

CHAPTER 9

Twists and Turns:
The Testing Phase

"Nothing in life is so exhilarating as to be shot at without result." —Sir Winston Churchill

hat we call the testing phase can start as soon as the first day back, or three or four weeks later. You'll recognize it when you see behaviors emerge that remind you of your *old* teenager. Obviously, when parents see this old teen appear, it triggers great anxiety, worry and possibly even anger on their part toward the teen and the whole treatment experience. It can trigger that parental post traumatic stress disorder (PPTSD). But forewarned is forearmed, and you need to expect this. Say it with me: "Hello, testing phase. I've been expecting you."

If there has ever been a time to manage your own emotions, it's now. This phase does not need to be made worse than it is. If

you handle this phase right, you will eventually be able to transition into the last and longest phase: the maintenance phase where things have settled into a more predictable routine. While the maintenance phase isn't perfect, you'll be less likely to experience heavy setbacks. In short, parents, buckle up. This is the most challenging phase of all.

First Signs

Any number of situations can signal the start of the testing phase, but the most common is some form of disrespect—for example, not accepting no for an answer or refusing to do something. On the extreme side, it can be drinking, sneaking out or drug use. We have seen teens drink alcohol, smoke marijuana or sneak a girlfriend into their beds the first night they were home, but remember, when challenges come rumbling forth again, it presents an opportunity for you as a parent to prove that things will be different than they were in the past. Each time you respond to a challenge, you define yourself as a parent, and each time you define yourself as a parent, you show your child (and yourself) what your family can and will be like. Parents, you are the leaders in the home, and it's your job to stay above the fray and above the emotional kinds of reactions that can pull you down to a level where you are no longer able to lead. Imagine if the program staff had taken things personally and jumped into a challenge with all of the fear, justification or frustration you have felt at an upset. It's your job to be in a good spot where you can continue to lead with wisdom, restraint and love.

There are several reasons we refer to this as a testing phase. First, sometimes teens will test you by breaking a rule, just to see if you will follow through as a parent. As a farm kid, I can tell you that it's just like moving cows into a new field: they will go around the perimeter of the fence and test it to see if there are any big holes or gates open. If there are even small holes or weaknesses in the fence, they will start pushing and squeezing until they get through. That's what teens do as well; they're checking to see if you're going to be able to follow through with those things you've discussed and the plans you've made.

Second, teens will test themselves. Teens are often skeptical about whether the skills they learned in all those hours of individual, group and family therapy will work for them in the real world. Sometimes they'll put themselves into a risky situation to see if they can handle being there without falling back into their old patterns—for example, going to a party where drugs or alcohol are present and not participating, or keeping their phone in their room without texting all night long.

The third reason for calling this a testing phase is that you, as parents, are learning new ways to handle things and are testing those approaches. You may have dabbled with the new skills, but with your struggling teen at home again, you are ramped up to high alert. You want to prove to yourself that you have the courage to follow through, even when it feels uncomfortable. Now this may sound very bold, but I firmly believe that it's more important for you as a parent to pass these tests than it is for

> Your response to this phase is in your control, even though you can't control how your teen will choose to test you.

your teen to pass them. I can almost hear you saying, "I hate that it is always my fault. Why do I have to be the one responsible for everything?" Understand, that's not what I am saying. As much as your teen needs to pass tests, you need to pass them even more. Your response to this phase is in your control, even though you can't control how your teen will choose to test you. How you respond will affect how long this phase lasts and how much damage occurs.

Never, Ever Say...

So when that initial defiant "No, I won't" hits you, how should you respond? My first suggestion is that you **never** say something along the lines of "Well, it's obvious you didn't change." What that does is put you immediately in a combative situation with your teen. It undermines all of the positive affirmations you've given your teen previously, and no matter what you say subsequently, your teen is just going to remember the hurtful thing you said. You're not going to have any positive influence when you do that, so under no circumstances should you fall back on that sort of retort because, let's be honest, it will only make matters worse.

Talk It Out

Make sure that you have someone to talk to in order to keep you from losing perspective, throwing your hands in the air and surrendering in defeat. As we discussed in Chapter 6 on the dangerous hidden waterfalls, you need someone who can help you see what's going well, someone who can encourage you and encourage your teen. Again, this can be a parent coach, a therapist, or someone from your home team. One teen who had experienced this kind of support during the testing phase told us, "I felt tons of encouragement from my coach. I think because our coach was so encouraging, my parents also became more encouraging about me, which helped a lot when I did go through the rough spots. I know it helped my mom feel calmer when she started to get anxious too." Having that outside voice of calm and steady validation or accountability, whichever one the case calls for, is going to keep you solid when you feel the earth starting to crumble. Flip back to the page where you listed the members of your home team. Has anyone else come to mind as you've continued to read and participate in the treatment journey?

Stay Calm and Hold the Boundary

The last suggestion here is to stay calm and hold the boundary. Follow through with consequences. A popular phrase from British World War II propaganda posters reminded the people to "Keep Calm and Carry On." It has recently become popular again, showing up on mugs, aprons, posters and puzzles, because it is an appropriate mantra for young and old, for wartime or for the battles you are engaged in today.

Here is a scenario that might give you some ideas on how to actually stay calm, hold the boundary, and follow through with consequences:

Two weeks after earning the use of his car, Sam left the school grounds with his friends for lunch and didn't make it back until the last period. His parents told him he would not be allowed to drive to school for one week. If he made up the truancy and went to all of his classes during the week, he would get his car back. Here are some of Sam's possible responses:

- "But I just lost track of time. This is so lame. No one else's parents do stuff like this." This possible response shows where he pushes your "need to be right" button.

- "It's my car and if you take my keys, then I'll break your lamp." Here he's using threats of physical violence to scare you into giving in to his demands.

- "You guys have such a double standard. You never take the car from Andy!" Now he's deflecting and hoping to make you focus on how unfair you are, rather than the fact that he broke the rules.

- "You're only doing this because Dad's making you. He's such a jerk. He doesn't see any of the good I'm doing. I know you're not this stupid, Mom." This is obviously Sam trying to split the two of you up, pitting one against the other so you question if being united is really the right thing here.

And here are some of the responses we've seen parents make:

- "That's because Andy never does the boneheaded things you do. It's like you haven't changed at all." We've already talked about what a no-no this would be.

- "Maybe we are being too hard on you. Okay, you can use the car, but don't let it happen again. We're trusting you." Here you are teaching Sam that he can cry unfair, and you will buckle, not holding the line when it comes to enforcing the consequence for the action.

- "Well, if that's your attitude we'll make it three weeks and now your phone is gone too." This is classic escalation. Don't turn the issue of missing school into an issue about the phone. Stick to the task at hand; resist piling on the punishments, because you can push your child to the point of giving up hope of ever getting what he or she wants and so will rebel against every rule.

- "I am sorry you feel that way. Nevertheless, that's our decision." Perfecto!

Of course the first three are common parent traps. The last shows consistency, calmness and confidence and offers a way to move forward from the teen's mishandled judgment call of that afternoon. If you didn't already do so, highlight the last bullet. This is a phrase we teach our parents to use to steady themselves in the moment, and to keep from shifting into lecture mode or a verbal battle. When one father used this phrase with his daughter, she replied, "Whenever a parent uses 'I'm sorry you feel that way, nevertheless,' a Homeward Bound coach earns his wings." We couldn't have agreed more or been more tickled.

Once the boundaries have been set, you need to be firm in your resolve not to shift the boundaries. You will undo the new pattern you are trying to establish with your teen with those slight shifts. It undermines their belief in your commitment to follow through. They need to believe things will automatically happen, without anger or malice, but that consequences will follow. They need to be able to rely on what you say, both on the freedoms they will receive for fulfilling their commitments and the negative consequences of breaking them. Say what you mean, and mean what you say. This follows your relationship even into adulthood. If you don't have a track record of follow-through now, there will come a time where you say you are going to let go or do something, and they won't respond because they've been led to believe you will capitulate or step back in and rescue them. For example "I won't fill out this college application for you, so get busy and get it done." If this is something you know you are going to end up doing anyway, don't make that threat. And even more difficult, but definitely more congruent, is to let the application deadline approach and pass.

Focus on *Your* Part

To do this you'll need to shift from a paradigm of "control" to a paradigm of influence. If you don't make this shift, you'll fall into power struggles and your son or daughter will likely fight against you even if the cost is great. Stay focused on your part and avoid these power struggles.

On the following page are questions to ask yourself to ensure the focus is where it needs to be.

At the risk of beating a dead horse, I keep coming back to this, but that's because it works. During the testing phase I encourage you to reach out to the home team of natural mentors. Remember, you've asked them to be a part of this treatment journey and transition home, so allow them to work their magic. Allow them to support you and your teen. When one mom couldn't roust her son out of the house to go to school, she simply called a friend who was a cop to come take the truant boy to school in his cop car. Another teen

Eleven Questions for Evaluating Challenging Moments

1. Did I stay calm and hold the boundary?

2. Did we stay unified as parents?

3. Did we keep ourselves from sliding into hopelessness and despair?

4. Did we follow through with appropriate consequences?

5. Which of my buttons did my son/daughter try to push? Was he or she successful?

6. Did we access our resources in an appropriate and helpful way?

7. What did we do well as parents? (What worked?)

8. What would I do differently if I could rewind the clock? (What didn't work?)

9. What was different (in a positive way) about our son or daughter's behavior?

10. What did we learn about our son or daughter as a result of the incident?

11. Overall, was I closer to being the type of parent I want to be?

threatened to take his truck out without his parent's permission, prompting Dad to simply call the neighboring farm manager who happily parked a tractor behind the truck, blocking it until calmer heads could prevail. When in doubt, stick with the solid principles you are learning through the treatment program and this book instead of flying off the handle and letting your emotions guide you. I promise you'll see better outcomes 100 percent of the time.

When You Need a Coach

My brother-in-law is an orthodontist by day but dreams of hanging out a shingle as a golf coach on his days off. He already has a steady stream of neighbors and buddies who will come to his back yard and hit ball after ball into a net while he carefully watches them and offers suggestions or tweaks to their form and follow-through.

As in any area of life that we try to improve, we must first admit to having blind spots. We understand how it's supposed to play out, and we subconsciously assign good motives and a real determination to our actions. Unfortunately, that's not always enough. Those blind spots can hamper our progress or ultimate success, every time. Parenting coaches shouldn't feel threatening. They can stand outside the swing and carefully, and unemotionally, watch you. They aren't there to judge you or condemn you but to tweak some things. They use their expertise and hours of watching families in the same situations to point out the strengths that they may not be capitalizing on, and at other times point out weak areas that need building up.

When do you need a coach or an expert? When you are faced with an important task, such as making changes to a long-standing family culture, a coach can steer you safely through the rapids. During the honeymoon phase, coaching is critical to keep you from falling into an "all is well" mentality, only to experience an emotional crash when you realize all is not well. But most especially, you need coaching during the testing phase. Otherwise, you will handle things as best you can on your own and desperately try not to go over the edge of a hopelessness, a threat-you-won't-follow-through-on, or a we-have-nowhere-to-turn waterfall.

When establishing value for transition services, one of the best things our coach would continually do for us was to remind us that there were going to be missteps, which there have been. His expert involvement and reassurance that one misstep does not mean the whole ball of twine is unraveling, is in the top two or three things he ever did for us. He would say, "It's not what the misstep is that's the important piece; it's can he get on back on track and how are we going to help him do it with our plan?" That was an incredibly valuable perspective, because without it, with that first bad day or bad choice, as a parent you are freaking out as to whether all of this past 18 months of wilderness and residential treatment was for naught. —PARENT (COLORADO)

Oh, absolutely. Our coach would use the word bump. 'Okay, it was a bump. Let's focus on what you are going to do with it as the parent.' —PARENT (LOUISIANA)

Never, Never, Never Give Up

This famous Winston Churchill quote is what I want to close this chapter with. Of all the useful information in this book, I'll bet that the chapter on the testing phase will be the most frequently reread. You will find yourself turning back to this section again and again to make sure you are doing all you can for this child who is struggling again or in a new way. I want you to remember to never lose hope, because the testing phase, just like the honeymoon phase, does end. Unfortunately, it tends to last a little longer than the honeymoon phase—yet there is an end to it. The fact is, kids eventually mature. Their brains finish developing. They start to understand boundaries better. They start to understand consistency, especially if they are not just reacting to your anger. They start to trust your love and wisdom. If you are able to calmly hold the boundary and place one foot in front of the other, continually pouring energy into the relationship, then the testing phase will end sooner rather than later. Either way, mistakes don't have to be fatal. They can be learning experiences, trial and error, repentance and forgiveness. You can always go back and ask for a "do-over" or a "take two" of the previous dramatic scene you acted out together. If a test is handled well, your teen will ultimately come to mirror your behavior in that his emotions will become calmer and more consistent, he will be more optimistic, and he will get to a place where his challenges are more like "normal" adolescent challenges.

Summary
CHAPTER 9: TWISTS AND TURNS: THE TESTING PHASE

- When the first signs of the *old* teenager reappear, you may feel a trigger of your Parental Post Traumatic Stress Disorder (PPTSD). Watch out for anxiety, worry, and possibly anger toward your teen and the whole treatment experience.

- When animals are turned out into a new field, they will test the boundaries looking for gates or holes in the fence to squeeze through to reach greener pastures. Your teens will be testing the boundaries in the same way.

- Remaining calm and holding the boundary is as much a test for you as it will be for your teen, who needs to be convinced that you say what you mean, and mean what you say.

- Find or hire a coach to steer you through the rough waters, to help you use strengths you may not be capitalizing on, or shore up your weak areas when they need reinforcement.

What to Do Now

Have a printed copy of your Family Rules and Consequences handy so you won't be caught in a moment of distraction or exhaustion and simply wing your response to the test. Perhaps you can keep a copy in your car or purse so it's always handy when you need your cheat sheet. Find a template to start building your own at www.NotbyChance.com.

CHAPTER 10

Win the Day:
The Maintenance Phase

"Persistent people begin their success where others end in failure." —Edward Eggleston

Football coach Chip Kelley teaches his players to win the day. He says that he doesn't focus on winning the National Championship, or even the game coming up next week. He reminds himself constantly that all he and the players need to focus on is winning the day. Some of you may be muttering under your breath, I'd be happy to win the hour, and I agree. So, let's not get ahead of ourselves!

With the rough air of the testing phase behind you, the maintenance phase begins. You may not recognize where testing stops and maintenance begins, because there will still be ups and downs and bumps, but they will be less severe than they were before. Internally, what's happening here is that your teen's confidence is increasing because he or she has been learning how to apply the coping skills that were learned in the treatment program and that you're helping nurture at home. Your child is seeing more success and is starting to connect more deeply and more often with the right people. He or she is feeling more comfortable in this new situation. Through these changes, your teen is taking hold of a new identity and a positive direction. The biggest hurdles of the transition are behind you, but this phase is not trouble-free. The key difference between the testing and the maintenance phase are, first of all, *you* are more confident; in fact that's how you'll know that you personally have reached the maintenance phase. Your confidence goes up when you've weathered the testing phase and come out the other side, just as your teen has done. Second, you'll discover that when you do come up against a challenge, you are able to stay calm and avoid overreacting. Your knowledge has increased. Your comfort level has increased. And your trust has probably increased too.

I love horse training, and I'm always surprised at the number of parallels there are between parenting and horse training. A particular quote I read by the well-known dressage instructor Mark Schaffer sticks in my mind. He said,

> The rider's [parent's] patience and knowledge run out at the same time. Once you know that, the next time you find yourself losing your patience with a horse [your teen], a little voice will go off in the back of your head saying, "You're just frustrated because you don't know what to do with this."

As we gain knowledge through wins and losses, our patience is going to increase as well. Just know that there is a light at the end of this tunnel. Let me share some suggestions for you during this maintenance phase.

Don't Kick Back

You may have the wonderful sense that things are calming down, so I must warn you again not to become complacent and forget to apply the principles that helped you get to this higher plateau in the first place. It's easy to take your hands off the wheel when things look like smooth sailing ahead. Obviously, you don't have to be on constant high alert during the maintenance phase, but you do need to remember there are some consistent principles that got you there. Don't let go of those now. We've seen parents so exhausted by the testing phase that when they got to this maintenance phase they took a big "attention vacation" and stopped monitoring their teen altogether. While it's certainly understandable, it's clearly a bad idea.

Expand the Privilege Pool

As your trust grows with each challenge met and conquered by your son or daughter, you have got to be ready to hand out the rewards before being asked. This does not mean just in the form of material goods or cash but in the expansion of your good will and trust. Remember this doesn't mean complete abdication of responsibility. Things can be handed out for a weekend trial, or at a level of 50

> **Be ready to hand out the rewards before being asked. This does not mean just in the form of material goods or cash but in the expansion of your good will and trust**

percent of what your child initially pushed for, without turning the whole show over to your teen's direction.

I understand how scary that can be to you. It's probably a little unnerving for your son or daughter as well. But if you are thoughtful and vigilant, you can rest assured that you have done what you can to prevent relapses and are doing the right thing to let your teen prove himself or herself. Parenting is always about knowing when to step back and let children make their own moves, whether they lead to a stumble or a tenuous but successful step.

Family Check-Ins

My next suggestion for you is to have continual family check-ins (daily is best; weekly is bare minimum) in order to keep your finger on the family pulse. Stay engaged in the family all the way through until your child is fully independent and you can safely let go.

What does a family check-in look like? That's completely up to you. You could simply review that day's upcoming activities over breakfast. Just be sure to start early enough to allow time to discuss conflicts or requests, without having to tear off to catch the train.

One suggestion as part of this Family Check-in is what we like to do monthly in our home. We call it a personal parent interview (PPI). Once a month, usually on a Sunday morning—because we are all more relaxed and have more free time then—we'll sit down in the den with each of our children individually and talk to them about their lives. It has actually become a very positive event for everyone; our youngest is always letting us know when it's his day for his PPI. What makes this a positive process for our family is that, first off, we are really listening to our children. They have the rare joy of the undivided attention of both parents. We shut the door and lock it so we don't have other kids coming in. We give them our eye contact and really attend to what they're saying. We ask questions such as: How is school going? What's your favorite class? What's the thing you're enjoying most about life right now? Tell us about your friends. Do you have a girlfriend? They love to talk and share what's happening in their lives, and they blossom with that focused attention. We work at keeping it light and positive, and we start asking the big questions while they are young so they aren't uncomfortable when they get to the age when questions such as What have you heard about drugs? and Do you have a girlfriend? are really relevant. Some teens don't want you snooping around their friends, but you can start out with nonthreatening questions, such as, Who's your best friend at school? Who's your best friend in our neighborhood? Who is your least favorite kid on the bus and why? Still thinking you want to play lacrosse this summer? If you have younger children, by all means give them your time and attention in this way too. The sooner you start communicating your values and your interest in your kids, the better the health of the entire family.

If you haven't done this kind of thing before, starting with your teen's transition from treatment to home is a perfect time. Call it a new tradition. Remember, it must be fun for you and for them, not heavy-handed and centered on problems. If you slip into lecture mode, get out of it quickly. You want these check-ins to be anticipated, not dreaded. One way we've kept them positive is to add to this check-in a small token monthly salary based on our children's performance of household and farm chores. This could sound like a lot, but it's not: $1 per year of age.

Granted, this is a pretty formal framework for a family check-in, but it's what works for us. There are lots of ways to give five minutes daily to listen to each one of your kids. Some parents find great success when they hold their check-ins in the car as they travel between school and extracurricular activities. It's a setting that brings everyone together in close proximity with some time spent. You aren't facing one another, but you have a captive audience. Tell a story from your day, which could prompt your kids to ask you questions. Then you could ask questions in return. Another option would be to gather for breakfast to discuss the upcoming day, or review the day at dinnertime. These check-ins can be held as a group occasionally, but should be held individually daily. Some of our best talks with our teens happen when we can barely prop our eyelids open. They are required to come and tell us they are home from their evening activities, and this late hour is when they happen to be the most open and animated.

One last tip: make sure all electronics are turned off so you can give your full attention to what is being shared. There is nothing more wonderful than being attended to by someone you love.

Stop the Volcano

When problems do occur, do not overreact. Here is what one mother reported to us after her son had been home for months. Notice how the parents and the son both did their part:

Certainly Todd's anger is a bad problem. I'm not denying it. But I think learning to defuse his anger by not reacting to it ourselves has really helped and you can see it working. It really is amazing. The other day he got mad about some stupid thing and when we just laid it out unemotionally, he stormed upstairs. In the old days there would have been door slamming and whatever. He was up there about five minutes, came down, did his thing, off he went and he is good as new. But we just never would have been able to do that before. —PARENT (MINNESOTA)

This is a simple example of the mother not overreacting to the presenting problem, which would have ballooned into a fight about disrespect, and instead, allowing her son the chance to take the time to work it out for himself.

My wife experienced the same thing as she was driving home one morning and decided to call ahead to have one of our sons get the mower out and start on the lawns. She told him that as soon as she arrived, she would grab the trimmer and together they'd have it all completed in 20 minutes—it was a small yard back then. He immediately started to whine and point out how he always had to do more than the other kids. He argued that it would take a lot more than 20 minutes, because she was always underestimating the time, and she should have had him do it the day before when he had more time.

Her natural instinct was to vehemently defend the appropriateness of her request and then to give him an earful on how much she does for the family without complaint, and so forth. You see where this could lead? Right when she was ready to let loose, a little thought came to mind, "Just be quiet." That was against everything she wanted to do right then. Fortunately, she decided to listen and keep quiet. When our son finished making his case, there was silence for about five seconds. She stayed on the line. Then, in a quiet voice, he said "Alright, I'll do it." By keeping her cool for just another moment, she allowed him time to think, come to grips with the request and realize it wasn't too much to ask. If she hadn't, the lawns would most likely have been done anyway, but there would have been a lot of tension and resentment for the rest of the day as well.

Have Fun

Some parents are all about fun. I want to use this moment to encourage the rest of us to loosen up. You have been through some very traumatic times as a family in pretreatment, in treatment and in the testing phase. You have to remind yourself to get engaged with what engages your children, whether that's playing computer games or going to a sporting event to cheer them on. Watch a movie they suggest and talk about it. Pull out the photo album or watch family videos together reliving the good times. Go shopping at a farmer's market rather than the grocery store for a new experience. All of us have busy lives, and all too often we excuse ourselves from being as engaged with our kids as we'd like to be. If this has been the case with your family, here is your chance to make good times a part of how you interact. Rediscover the pleasure of family mealtime without your cell phone on the table. Give attention to the details in your children's lives, not just the fires.

Certainly, I understand that in some families that have faced really daunting challenges, the parents may be so traumatized that they are reading this and thinking, "My kid can't even stand to have me in the same room, much less play checkers with me or put up with a formal check-in." But some of the ideas may be the ice-breaker you need, so just keep an eye open for the right moment and grab it. You're not going to be able to do everything I've suggested here, of course, so pick and choose what works for your family and don't get overwhelmed by it. Start by taking your kid on an errand or to a scheduled activity, rather than relying on the nanny or the carpool. You can stop for a bite to eat, or ask your kid's advice

> Give attention to the details in your children's lives, not just the fires.

on what to do for Grandma's birthday. It gets easier and easier to include one another in your lives.

Plan Ahead to Connect

What are your plans for tomorrow? Of those "to-do's," in which one or two of them could you include your teen?

1.

2.

3.

And so on ...

Summary
CHAPTER 10: WIN THE DAY: THE MAINTENANCE PHASE

- There will still be bumps throughout this phase, but they will be less severe than before.

- Your confidence, as well as your teen's coping skills will both increase as you've made it through the rough waters of the testing phase.

- Establish a routine for family check-ins. These few minutes daily will keep you engaged and aware of the thoughts and needs of your teen. Don't drop off your teen's radar simply because things look good from afar.

- As in the other three phases, keep an eye on your own actions and reactions. Maintain your label as influencer, rather than drill sergeant or buddy.

What to Do Now

Privately commit to spending a minimum of seven minutes with each of your children daily. Ask about their day and share some of the details of yours. Acknowledge, laugh and love in those short moments. They will become the highlights of the day for all of you.

CHAPTER 11

No Such Thing as Luck: Helping Your Teen Keep the Momentum

"We first make our habits, and then our habits make us." —JOHN DRYDEN

In taking a leisurely ride with my horse on an equestrian trail near our home, we came upon a tunnel that ran under the street. Howdy, my buckskin quarter horse saw it from far off and knew he didn't want to go near it—dark, enclosed places are terrifying to many animals. In the past I would have believed I needed to force him through that dark passage, with me on his back. After all these years the words of my father and the words of his father automatically repeated in my mind, "Show him who's the boss. You can't let him do what he wants to do." As powerful as old scripts are to counteract, I insisted on making myself predisposed to the more helpful advice I have picked up as an adult: "He's just afraid. He's not trying to be belligerent or the boss." I knew from watching myself over the years that my pattern was to get intense and uptight with my horse when he balked or became skittish. Bad outcomes and updated education taught me that I needed to manage myself before I had the slightest chance of turning this situation into a learning experience rather than a rodeo. I continued with the self-talk, "Encouragement and small steps are what he needs to get through this, and he can do this." I knew the outcome I sought might take a while longer, but showing patience and allowing time now would shape the future of our relationship for the better. I knew if I had gone "old school," as my automatic reactions were inviting me to do, or even "new school," which could have sounded something like "This is too much to ask of my horse. I'll find a route that works for him," the results would have been somewhere between totally unsatisfying and traumatic. From then on every time he came to a tunnel, he would have felt incapable of facing it. Fear would have gripped him and he would have frozen up and probably thrown me off if I had persisted.

Instead, I stopped and let him look at the tunnel from a distance. Then I coaxed and encouraged him. Not wanting his anxiety to go through the roof, I tried to get the other horses and riders to go through first so he could follow. His buddies didn't want to go in either, so before he became frustrated and did something dangerous, I "got off his back" and led the way through. With me leading, and a little tug here and there, he came through, scared to death—choppy steps, tense muscles, flared nostrils—but with the other horses tentatively coming along right behind him.

I knew I had handled the whole thing well and it made me smile. I had a feeling of empowerment followed by the very strange realization that I could hardly wait for the return trip back through the tunnel. I believed I would see definite progress.

On the return, as the tunnel came into view, Howdy's ears were erect and facing forward, his eyes studying the dark hole intensely. He slowed but never faltered as he made his way up to and through the tunnel. His confidence soared. I stroked his neck and spoke to him, "See, that wasn't so scary" letting him know he had done well.

I chose to use the same patience and follow this same pattern with everything he had balked at on the way out. We were both learning and enjoying the experience. I didn't force him; I just encouraged him and took my time and was patient. Most things he worked through himself (the hammering of roofers, plastic sacks that had blown into the fence and slats from a privacy fence that had blown down onto the path). I gave him wide berth around those fears, all the while encouraging him to get closer each time. On the way back home, he didn't even blink.

Stretch Goals

Coming out of a program, your teen has started a track record of success. He or she has overcome some challenges and has grown within the safety of the program. Progress going forward will depend on continuing to stretch and move through the tunnels. Each challenge will require your teen to overcome one or more demotivating emotions that stand in the way. Fear, discouragement, sad moods, disappointments, anger and lack of motivation will all rear their ugly heads. At times they will seem insurmountable. Your job will be to gently encourage your teen to go forward. Remind your child of past successes while expecting him or her to continue putting one foot in front of the other, even if he or she can only muster tentative steps.

Your teen now has a base of confidence built upon achievements that previously couldn't have been imagined.

Have realistic expectations of your teen. If you expect things that are too far out of your teen's knowledge base, comfort zone or belief in himself or herself, you are setting them up for failure. Be patient and introduce some stretch goals, something a little beyond your child's comfort zone but not too far outside it. An engaged parent leads the way as a role model. Show how it can be done. Teach how to eat an elephant, one bite at a time. When your teen reaches that goal, barriers will start to come down in their own mind and he or she will reach for new things. Success first comes as a surprise and then as a habit.

> Success first comes as a surprise and then as a habit.

Call on the Home Team

When we find ourselves locking horns with our teens, and they aren't motivated because it is *we* who are asking it of them, try asking home team members to find ways to get them to keep moving. For example, one of my sons is pretty timid around our horses, having been dumped in the dirt and traumatized on several occasions. When one of his friends, a Future Farmers of America (FFA) council member needed to borrow a horse for the summer stock parade, my son invited himself along on the ride with us. With his peer present, I asked my son if he would like to ride Joe, our tallest horse and one he had never ridden before. He jumped right up on him and handled him with poise and confidence, even taking him to a trot at times. I watched in amazement at the power of friends for instilling confidence and motivation in someone I hadn't been able to inspire with all of my brilliant—but ineffective—therapeutic and persuasive powers.

Motivating Teens

We all know you can lead a horse to water, but you can't make him drink. You can see him hot and sweating, yet you aren't able to make him partake of what would help him. Motivating anybody comes from within. In his book *Drive: The Surprising Truth about What Motivates Us*, Daniel Pink teaches that it is a deeply human need to direct our own lives, to learn and create new things and to do better by ourselves and our world. For instance, "We leave lucrative jobs to take low-paying ones that provide a clearer sense of purpose. We work to master the clarinet on weekends although we have little hope of making a dime or acquiring a mate from doing so. We play puzzles even when we don't get a few raisins or dollars for solving them."

In what way or area does your teen show signs of self-motivation? Encourage him or her to run with it, but be careful not to get so excited about this positive development that you take over and try to become the coach or boss in their new game. Motivation that has sprouted from the teen themselves, has it's best chance of growth if you leave them as the gardener.

Relapse Prevention Plan

Relapse prevention is a huge component of any addiction recovery program and should be part of the aftercare process following treatment for any malady. Many of the same concepts apply whether we are talking about avoiding relapse into drug use or relapsing into old ruts of depression, for example. In each case there will be factors that induce relapse, such as high-risk situations, poor coping skills, lack of support and so forth.

With drug and alcohol relapse, or sex or gaming addictions, you have a fairly specific behavior that you are trying to overcome and there are usually many red flags along the way before a person crosses the line. Although sometimes more difficult to identify, the same is true with other behaviors we are trying to extinguish, such as disrespect, refusal to attend school, depression, and so on. A relapse prevention plan is meant to teach people how to identify the red flags that indicate a slide toward the problem behavior and give them strategies for managing them early to avoid a full relapse.

To download a Drug and Alcohol Relapse Plan template go to www.NotbyChance.com. From this plan you will be able to craft something similar for whatever behavior you are trying to help your teen avoid in the future.

School Success Plan

For most parents, school is never very far from their thoughts. Their program undoubtedly had teachers or academic counselors who helped their teens chip away at requirements for school credit. They have most likely met with the school administrator or counselors in their hometown to register their sons or daughters for their return to school. There may be online packets that need to be completed for a GED or high-school diploma to be awarded, or for SAT/ACT tests to be taken for college applications. Resources are available to you in the form of academic coaches, study buddies and summer school. Feel free to download the School Success Plan we use from www.

NotByChance.com to ensure you are keeping on track with individualized education programs (IEPs) or graduation requirements.

Daily Schedule

Everyone loves a holiday. To break from routine can be a relief for both a teen and an adult. However, if a holiday continues for too long, it will quickly lapse into the doldrums. Boredom and trouble begin to brew in the absence of structure and contribution.

I suggest that while your teen is still in the program, you submit a suggested daily schedule that the program staff and therapist can go over and tweak together, even before your teen returns home. This can list bedtimes and wake-up times, meals, time for household chores, time for academics, time for employment, and time for fun/relaxation. Though these daily schedules will need enough flexibility to make them sustainable, they will also need to be firm enough that expectations and freedoms can be maintained through their use.

Exercise

I don't know of any adolescent treatment program that doesn't have exercise built into its structure. Whether training for triathlons, practicing yoga, or moving through the ranks of karate, program designers take account of the importance of physical exertion in beating the blues and in keeping participants engaged and healthy. Some teens are already very physically active, and others will need to be prodded. Build into the schedule a variety of ways to keep your teen moving physically every day of the week.

A 2006 study (Hallal et al. 2006) in *Sports Med* showed that higher levels of sport participation and physical activity were related to lower levels of depression and that exercise can contribute to better self-perception. There are many other benefits including increased energy, better bone health, decreased obesity and fewer health problems such as cancer and heart disease.

All Right Everybody ... Get Moving!

Here are some beginning ideas to help you start jotting down a few of your own:

- ☐ Sign up for a gym membership together, and maybe have a friend do the same.

- ☐ Participate in a walk or run to raise awareness for a cause.

- ☐ Revisit a team sport that your teen was involved in as a child.

- ☐ Assign your teen to walk the dog and go along yourself.

- ☐ On vacation try something new such as hiking, skiing, snorkeling, biking or a Zumba class. Since your teen won't know the other participants in these activities, he or she will be less likely to feel self-conscious if you are there too.

Sleep Patterns

Early to bed and early to rise—experts say that a teen should be getting between eight and a half to more than nine hours of sleep each night. We often see overscheduled teens who get far less than that between school, extracurricular activities and a full night of homework. What time they might find in between is often snatched up by their addictions to the television, computer, cell phones, or music. "I need it. I can't fall asleep without it!" they will often wail when we try to shut things down. Sleep deprivation is a major factor in bringing on depression, or relapsing into drug use or oppositional and defiant behaviors. Read *Snooze ... or Lose* by Dr. Helene Emselem to be convinced, or simply observe how effective you are in your own relationships or your day job when you haven't had enough sleep— the downward spiral starts. It's hard to separate what is truly bad in your life from what is simply caused by sleep deprivation. Do not let bad habits slip back in because you don't want to address a subject your teen will emphatically disagree with you on. If sleep is a key to your teen's success, create boundaries to encourage sleep. Help your teen keep a healthy sleep pattern, and you will see an improvement in optimism, an uptick in overall health and skyrocketing motivation.

Employment

Work is an accomplishment and brings satisfaction. It brings interactions with the community. It also brings the all-important dollar. Home team members may be able to help your teen find a suitable after-school or weekend job; ask around. Discuss and decide upon how many hours a week your teen may work during the school year, and help him or her make a budget for spending and saving toward college or independent living. If your goal, as a parent, is to raise an independent, healthy, functional and contributing member of society, it goes without saying that you must make a plan to find your teen work outside your home.

Service

Thinking beyond the self is a trait few teens are known for. It's not that they are genuinely selfish or inherently evil; they are just preoccupied with the changes and challenges they face. Young teens' capacity for empathy is limited by brain development as well. Nurturing an interest in service until they come to enjoy the good feeling they get, or giving them a break from their own concerns can be a welcome distraction while at the same time teaching them that contributing to something beyond themselves offers big dividends in self-esteem and happiness. Service will teach the value that other people and their needs are every bit as important as their own. It is something you hope every adult, every marriage partner, parent or coworker understands. The benefits that service will bring throughout your teen's life are too many to count.

I'm Off to Work

List three people with whom you and your teen can discuss employment opportunities:

☐ A peer who works somewhere you'd like to;

☐ Family friends who use teens in their businesses;

☐ An organization or business that interests you for a future career.

Let Me Help with That

Here are some potential service opportunities to start your own ideas churning:

- ☐ Serve a meal at the local soup kitchen.

- ☐ Visit a nursing home, whether you have relatives there or not, and hand out cards of encouragement or a holiday token.

- ☐ Practice random acts of kindness in your home for a week, and then share what you did at a special culminating dinner.

- ☐ Write letters to loved ones far away, to encourage, congratulate or just ask after them.

- ☐ Take a trash bag to collect litter the next time you take a walk in your neighborhood.

- ☐ Volunteer to read stories to children at your local library.

- ☐ Add three more of your own ideas.

Hobbies and Play

This area of life needs to include more than video gaming or shopping at the mall. Use hobbies and play to set a nonthreatening and fun stretch goal. In doing so, you will remember why you like each other. Sometimes your inexperience will allow your teen to teach you and you can both laugh at your mistakes. Plato wisely stated, "You can discover more about a person in an hour of play than in a year of conversation."

Just for Fun

Introduce your teen to something new that neither of you have any experience in. Hand your teen this list and say, "You choose five and I'll choose five. We'll see where we cross over, and commit to trying one of these together this weekend."

☐ Digital photography
☐ Building a simple robot
☐ Free-style rapping
☐ Longboarding
☐ Geocaching
☐ Cartooning
☐ Barbequing
☐ Container gardening
☐ Graphic design
☐ Jewelry making
☐ Mosaics
☐ Poetry reading
☐ Calligraphy
☐ Knitting or needlework

☐ Hacky sac
☐ Ultimate Frisbee
☐ Origami
☐ Hair styling
☐ Scrapbooking
☐ Blogging
☐ Pen pals
☐ Tennis
☐ Ham radios
☐ Hunting
☐ Outdoor concerts
☐ Foreign films
☐ Opera
☐ Fly tying

Social Interactions

Your teen has been interacting with a wide range of people during treatment. Not only were there professionals and staff your teen had to communicate with, but there were roommates and challenging activities and social situations that your teen learned to navigate. You may picture your child as shy or struggling, but having been away for a time, your child has undoubtedly learned to move through uncomfortable situations and find friendship and fun wherever possible. Even if your child rolls his or her eyes at your suggestions or calls them "lame," keep the interactions happening. Samuel Johnson said, "If a man does not make new acquaintances as he advances through life, he will soon find himself alone. A man, sir, must keep his friendships in constant repair."

Out and About

Here are some social activity ideas to start your own wheels turning:

☐ Go to church/synagogue/mosque.

☐ Host a hang-out or party for them.

☐ Invite one of their peers along on a family outing.

☐ Go camping with neighbors, allowing them to show off some wilderness skills.

☐ Visit a zoo with a younger niece or nephew.

☐ Attend the sporting or musical event of a sibling or friend.

☐ Encourage your teen to ask someone to the school dance.

☐ Have your teen do the grocery shopping for one meal or for the week.

☐ List three more of your own ideas here.

Energy begets energy. The most productive people are often the happiest. When you think of what a program has to do to make sure there isn't too much downtime, which can lead to regression or stagnation, hold yourself to the same kind of commitment at home, even if it's to a much lesser level.

Summary
CHAPTER 11: NO SUCH THING AS LUCK:
HELPING YOUR TEEN KEEP THE MOMENTUM

- Moving teens through new challenges at home will help maintain the momentum they've gained in treatment. Stretch goals will keep the confidence, excitement and progress mounting.

- If drugs and alcohol were a problem before treatment, help your son or daughter create a relapse prevention plan to avoid the people, places and moods that accompanied drug/alcohol use.

- Knowing how to handle the challenge of your youth's academic career, through tutors, online help or regular meetings with the school counselor, will keep your goals at the forefront. Having accountability present more often than just when report cards come out is key to maintaining momentum.

- Consistent structure in your teen's daily schedule, exercise, sleep patterns, employment, service opportunities, hobbies and social interactions will amount to a well-rounded and healthy son or daughter.

What to Do Now

Flip back through this chapter and pick one of the boxes to experiment with.

CHAPTER 12

Your Turn: Parenting–The Number-One Thing Within Your Control

"I wanted to change the world. But I have found that the only thing one can be sure of changing is oneself." —ALDOUS HUXLEY

T
wo years ago, we bought a new English/American bulldog for our kids, to replace a dog that we had to put down because of cancer. We wanted so desperately to "do it right" this time in regard to his training. We needed all of the kids—and ourselves as parents—on the same page to make sure we were training him correctly. This was brought into sharp focus because we were buying Jeeves from a guy who really knew what he was doing. He was an expert in training police dogs

in Australia, and his love for the animals and for this breed inspired us to want to do everything perfectly. We had a golden opportunity, so we determined to be the best family this dog could have asked for. We educated ourselves thoroughly on the subject: we read books, watched videos and interviewed people who had dogs that were well behaved. From Jeeves' first night home, to the food, exercise, commands, boundaries and all the rest, we were deliberate. We had no control over the dog's genetics, or personality or smarts, but with deliberate and clear direction, we could learn what it took to help him achieve his potential as a family pet.

If I had had my second child first I would have thought, "Wow, I am such a fine parent" because we are on the same wavelengths. My first one just sees the world so differently from how I see it and that is always going to be a challenge for us. However, it also makes life interesting. —PARENT (SOUTH DAKOTA)

When you have children, you get what you get, as far as the personality they come with. You can't take the blame or the credit for it. Your teen's treatment and transition back to your home is as clean a parenting slate as you can get with someone in their teens. These transitions rarely happen in a lifetime, but your son or daughter and your entire family is knocking on the door of something potentially wonderful. A second chance at your family's health and relationships is a blessing most will never receive and I want to help you maximize it.

We have spent the previous chapters talking about my experience in the field of adolescent treatment, what good programs look like, how to make the most of the treatment experience, the dangers waiting after discharge and the four phases of transition. Now I want to deliver an empowering pep talk.

> **Your teen's treatment and transition back to your home is as clean a parenting slate as you can get with someone in their teens.**

Circle of Influence

After what you have read, I hope you are feeling educated and ready to run with it. There is no need to feel helpless or hopeless. There is a powerful principle taught by Stephen Covey in his book *Seven Habits of Highly Effective People*. He talks about the circle of influence and the circle of concern. Let's use this precept to talk about your role as a parent. The circle of concern is a large circle that symbolically encompasses all of the things that a parent might be concerned about in this transition to home. Inside that larger circle is a smaller inner circle that encompasses only the things that parents actually have influence over, so it's called the circle of influence.

Fundamentally, all of our concerns will fall within the larger circle of concern, but some of them are special and fall within our circle of influence. Covey teaches that there is great power in being able to identify which ones are within the smaller circle of influence. We can then put our energy and focus into the area of influence. What happens when we do that? Well, our influence over our

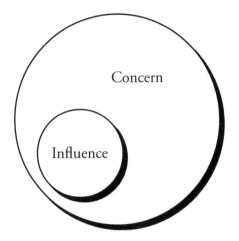

concerns grows, bringing more of our concerns under our influence. I want you to understand that it's not too late to actively remake your parenting style, to redefine yourself as a parent and to affect this relationship and this transition. All of these things fall within your circle of influence, which is about you and your parenting, and how you manage this situation that's unfolding with your teen's return. The transition will then come more under your circle of influence.

Promise me, and more importantly, yourself, that you will be 100 percent present with your teen and with what you want to accomplish at home.

Use blinders, like the ones they use on horses pulling carriages in the city, so that the things you can't control won't distract you. Do not look too far ahead or you'll become overwhelmed with the distance left in accomplishing your goals. Execute your plan with the great hope and confidence that your part will be significant. Let go of the rest. The parenting principles over the next few pages will help you do that.

1. Parenting Leadership Is Essential to Healthy Families.

If you don't provide the structure and leadership inside the walls of your home, who will? I can guarantee that if you leave it up to teens, they're not going to create the appropriate level of structure for their maturity. If you need help creating that structure, ask for it. Your son or daughter should not be expected to be able to maintain the gains he or she has made, when set adrift without appropriate boundaries. Things will atrophy, leading your child right back to where he or she was before.

Remember not to try extending the honeymoon by failing to correct or impose consequences when needed. Our children rely on that framework.

We had some problems with one of our own teens missing curfew night after night. He explained that he didn't mean to constantly arrive a half-hour late; it was just that he'd be talking and forget to check his watch. My wife and I consulted one another and decided that we had to set some reasonable consequences. It was easy to come up with those when we were angry at him—which is not the time to come up with a consequence. When he finally did come in, we calmly told him that he would lose an hour of his curfew time the next weekend he was late. Miracle of miracles—he started making it home on time, creating a positive track record. In other words, the first time he kept curfew didn't mean that we'd immediately loosen up on those consequences. We had stipulated a specific amount of time of doing well before the privilege was given back. As we provided the clear leadership and the expectations that would hold him accountable, he started to have consistent success. Soon we were able to come together and say, "Hey, it's time to give you more time with your friends; you have earned it. We really appreciate you honoring our agreement." We could see that he felt a little better about himself as it sunk in that our trust in him was being restored.

Also, remember that teens are expert at flipping the leadership hierarchy. Our Homeward Bound parents think we're practically prophetic when we hear what was happening before treatment and make predictions, almost with a timeline, of how quickly the teen will try to do "the flip." There's nothing prophetic about it; it's just that we've seen it over and over again.

If teens used violence or running away to get their way, it's only a matter of time before they pull those big guns out again, because they know it worked before. It has been said that leadership is being able to keep your head when everyone around you is losing theirs. That is certainly what is required in parenting as well. So, take the "happiness thermometer" out of your teen, if you are constantly checking your child's emotional temperature (which ends up affecting your temperature as well), and stick it into something you have real control over, such as your own actions, your own health, your hobbies or your family leadership role. Stay calm, set expectations and allow your teen to choose to follow them or not.

2. Nurturing the Relationship is a Priority.

I list this principle as second in importance, because as you are establishing, or re-establishing, the hierarchy in the home, it's important to remember that people will only follow leaders they respect, trust and love. Sometimes the only reason your teen will do as you ask is because he or she loves you.

If your teen has been away in treatment for months or even years, it has been a very long time since you were interacting directly and permanently with your teen in the home. Before treatment, you may have struggled with your anger or frustration or feelings of utter helplessness regarding your teen. At it's worst, these moments may have even caused you to say things that severely damaged the relationship or even made you feel that you didn't love your child. You may have deliberately withdrawn your love. But that never teaches a lesson or drives a point home. It only invites more of the very thing we do not want: resistance. We have less influence as a parent, and a lot more of this vicious cycle.

Aaron

I worked with Aaron and his parents in Chicago. He had some slight learning disabilities and emotional regulation problems. Though he was normally a sweet guy, he would become overwhelmed and have extreme and violent blow-ups at school, cussing and even threatening to hit a teacher. They lived in a tightly knit community and he attended a religious private school. His loss of control caused a lot of shame for the family.

His father, George, believed that if his son was not obeying some of the core rules of the family, he shouldn't show him any love or affection. Aaron was eventually kicked out of the school, and Dad decided to punish Aaron by not speaking to him until all was rectified and Aaron was back in school. Aaron started acting out more. He desperately wanted his dad to feel good about him, but because of the pressure cooker he was in, and because he wasn't getting any kind of positive feedback from his father, he became more anxious, angrier and more emotionally and behaviorally deregulated. Before they knew it, six months had passed and George had not so much as said, "Good morning," to a son he loved. They were stuck and their educational consultant called us for help

As I worked with the family, my primary goal was to help George question his assumption about how to help and influence his son. Within a short time he not only began speaking to Aaron but he also began to actively look for the good in his son, rather than only focusing on the shame his son had brought to the family. Before long, George started to take his son with him on trips and they began doing some of the things they'd enjoyed together in the past. True to his sensitive and kind nature, Aaron quickly forgave his father for the way his father had treated him over those long months.

It's crucial that you work proactively to build a new connection of love and warmth and friendship. There are appropriate ways to rebuild that relationship of trust without saying, "I made a mistake in sending you away." Almost always, the relationship is poor before the teen goes into treatment, so now you need to rebuild the relationship by becoming a great detective and expert on what registers as a loving action or gesture to your teen. Gary Chapman's *The Five Love Languages* explains that all of us have different ways of experiencing love from other people. What makes *us* feel loved may be different from our son's or daughter's love language. Would a thoughtful little gift such as a new soccer ball or a favorite candy bar be the best way to express your love? Maybe it's best expressed via a hand-written love note. Or is it a rough and tumble wrestle on the floor, or a back scratch during a movie or before bed?

Lastly on this point, there are natural shifts as a teen matures. Parents' need for connection is not the same as their teens' need. Teens move from idolizing parents, to seeing parents as fallible people who make mistakes. They need their parents, but they want to be independent of them. Their mistakes are much more costly and long-term. They are trying to cut the apron strings right at the time their parents feel their wisdom and experience as good students, dependable employees, or trusted friends could be most helpful. Though parents would like to hold on to their children, the relationship is changing. A beautiful quote from a Richard Paul Evans book, *The Christmas Box*, describes a father watching his darling young daughter. Part of him wishes he could keep her that way forever, but he admits that, as in music, "To hold the note would spoil the song."

3. Clear Expectations Encourage Consistency and Teach Values.

When our forefathers convened to draft a constitution for this new nation, the United States of America, the plan was to create something that would stand as a guide for the people and their government forever. It was not intended merely to guide us through the launch phase, or the transition from England's rule. It was based on true principles that would stand the test of time, could flex when the need arose and could be referred to over and over again as new questions would arise. Every family should have its own constitution, explaining the family's values, expectations, responsibilities and rewards. Some families create something more like a mission statement, and though there are differences, it is generally the same idea.

Just as training our puppy called for love and consistency, establishing a home where there are clear expectations of behavior and contribution with a promise of appropriate freedoms and love provides conditions under which teens will thrive. You have an advantage if you have sent your teen to treatment; you showed your child by doing so that you are serious about your expectations. You need to continue the same line of thinking now.

Do not be swayed into changing your expectations or your family constitution based on what everyone else is doing. I can't count how many times I've said, "I know your friends had a cell phone at eight years old, but that's not how we do it in our home. Our expectations are something different." The reality is it's common for parents to feel they're the only ones setting the boundaries, because teens will often claim that no other parent on the planet says no to R-rated movies, or to underage drinking parties. We may tend to believe them, because we haven't been in their friends' homes and they have. But if you remain firm in your expectations and values because they are right for your family, you will provide them with a road map in a world where values are adrift. In many cases, these values will be ones that the teens will subscribe to as they raise their own families in years to come. So if you feel yourself weakening, think of the future generations that will depend on your wisdom when they are pitted against their own teens' insistence.

A quick example here: I worked with a mom who was fearful about setting expectations about dress standards for her daughter, Cherie. Until the time when we worked with this family, following her return from a wilderness program, Cherie had pretty much called the shots on what her wardrobe would be. But when she came home, after her parents put their heads together and decided to be united on this topic, they decided to tighten up the dress standards and ask her to wear clothes that were less revealing. Lest you think they were being too prudish, the whole time I was in their home, this girl wore a flash-dance-type sweatshirt with almost one whole cup of her bra hanging out. This happened with a professional in the home, so imagine what it would have been like if she'd dressed down! For the parents, the issue was, at least in part, one of safety. Her provocative clothing sent an inappropriate and potentially dangerous message, which happened to be the area in which Cherie wanted the most freedom.

My advice to Mom was to continue to share her values with Cherie without lecturing and to hold her expectations steady while Cherie lived in her house. This meant defining clearly what "appropriate" looked like. It was very difficult for Cherie's parents to hold such standards when all the girls in school—according to Cherie—were wearing the same revealing clothing. But they stuck with them, and ultimately, their daughter complied, choosing more modest clothing than she had in the past. While I'm certain that Cherie didn't ever really buy in 100 percent, she respected her parents' wishes while she was in their home. Was this just a hoop to jump through, and was it a waste of their efforts? In my opinion, no, it was not a waste. If you have a strong sense of what is right, a value about something, and you set expectations about it, you are clarifying that value for your children. You are living with integrity. Your children may not internalize the same values as you, but that doesn't mean you can't still teach those values. At least Cherie knows that every time she wears something that is too short, too low or too tight Mom has higher standards than that. Again, the hope is that as they get older and more mature, teens will understand why these rules existed and they'll try to teach their kids the same things.

As parents we try to model good and acceptable behavior. Defining our expectations is one thing; making sure that our actions are consistent with our words is another. Nothing will nullify our words more quickly than continually falling short of the standards ourselves. I know this from personal experience regarding driving safety. I always buy cars that want to go fast. These cars are just made that way. I blame it on my mom allowing my brother and me to buy an orange Trans Am as teenagers. One of my justifying thoughts for my "adult driving habits" is that I'm now more mature and have had years of driving experience. I've practiced going fast for 30 years now. But it's not a value of mine to go fast; it's a bad habit. The value that I really want to instill in my children is to be law-abiding citizens and to be careful in driving. Well, I'm not always congruent with that. When my kids were young, they didn't check my speedometer against the speed limits posted along the highway. They are now old enough to do so. Every time I see my son back out of our long driveway like a bat out of you-know-where, I have two emotions. One is anger that he could be so careless, and the other is guilt that I have done the same thing and he has watched me do it.

4. Choice and Accountability Invite Growth.

As I have mentioned in previous chapters, our teens need to be able to prove that they can make appropriate decisions if they are to continue to grow and mature. Though parents are often hesitant to provide options, fearing their children will choose differently from their hoped-for choice, if they do not offer the freedom to choose, power struggles are sure to ensue.

One of the most helpful parts of a treatment program is that teens have been accountable for their choices to staff, to peers, to their therapist and to the program rules. They are learning that they aren't an island, and their actions reverberate. A significant precedent has already been set, so parents need to continue to hold their sons or daughters accountable in appropriate ways. They should not undermine what has been constructed by rescuing their children rather than letting their children account for their actions or behavior.

Let me make it clear: not all accountability needs to be in the form of a consequence. The better scenario by far is when teens have the maturity to hold themselves accountable and have their own goals to strive for. Mom and Dad, be careful that in your quest to "help" them you don't take that over for them. For example, two of our sons who played on the same soccer team wanted to become better players, so they took it upon themselves to register for early-morning conditioning sessions. I was really tempted, since I was usually awake at that time of day, to go upstairs, shake them awake and warn them that they were going to miss the practice if they didn't get going. But I knew that all that would accomplish would be teaching them that they didn't have to set their own alarms. Still, I really wanted them to go early to improve their soccer game and become more confident. Fortunately, I held myself back from becoming their wake-up call. After they missed a few of these voluntary practices, something clicked and they took the initiative to set their alarm clocks. Kids can learn to hold themselves accountable without parents acting as a cattle prod. In this case the positive peer pressure and desire for glory on the field was all they needed.

One more reminder: select consequences to match the behavior. Don't overdo or underdo the punishment and don't forget that positive consequences must follow when behaviors or actions warrant that kind of attention. I believe it is sometimes more helpful to assign a smaller punishment because it is one you are more likely to follow through with. It should be uncomfortable for the teen but not devastating. Think fly swatter, rather than sledge hammer.

In training horses, for example, you have to be careful that the correction you set for a horse—which is usually just a little more pressure on the horse's flank one way or the other—is not coming out of anger, intimidation or force. If it is, you are going to lose that relationship. The horse will start to mistrust you and become skittish around you, wondering where you're coming from. Again, with your teen, you need to cultivate a very calm, controlled leadership style.

5. Parental Unity Creates Family Stability and Strength.

If you could see me, you'd see my face is blue because I've talked about this topic so often, but it's because if unity isn't functional—well, you know what they say about a house divided. If you've got one parent who is doing his or her job and being consistent, but the other one is either laissez-faire or extreme in his or her parenting style—or just totally disengaged—parental unity breaks down.

Teens become very adept at finding that gap and learning to split parents wide enough apart to get past them. Here are four common tactics teens use to split parents apart:

a. "Mom said it's okay with her if it's okay with you" (when Mom actually hasn't said yes);

b. Asking for permission to do something from the parent who doesn't know that the teen is grounded;

c. Cornering or badgering the more lenient parent when the firm parent is not around;

d. Asking a parent to keep a secret from the other parent ("but please don't tell Dad").

Not being involved in the crisis yourself, you should be able to see how damaging each of those tactics can be. They probably also sound quite familiar. But kids aren't the only ones to split parents apart. Sometimes we do it to ourselves.

   a. "I" talk: constantly using "I" instead of "we" when sharing your parenting decision with your children;

   b. Throwing your co-parent under the bus: "Your mom thinks you shouldn't go out, but I don't really care. I'll leave it up to her."

   c. The reversal: "I know your dad said you couldn't go out tonight, but you did do your homework, so I think it will be alright."

   d. Open criticism: "I wish your mom would stop nagging all of us so much."

   e. Open disagreements: Talking in front of the children about marital and parental disagreements.

Teens, like water, will take the path of least resistance. A farmer who has plowed and prepared a new field with furrows for irrigation knows this firsthand. Ignoring this fact will lead to the failure of his farm. In the early spring he prepares the soil by plowing or loosening the dirt; he levels it and then forms straight rows for seeds to be planted in and furrows to turn the water in. Before the water hits it, the dirt is soft and there are always weaknesses in the rows, such as low spots or clods of dirt that dam the furrow, making it easy for the water to wash out the rows and seeds. All of these weaknesses will be exposed as the water starts coming down the row. A wise farmer knows that on his first few watering turns, he must "tend" the water carefully, making sure it reaches the end of the row. Once the water has made it down the row successfully a couple of times, the furrow is formed, with the dirt now crusted and formed into a harder mud, so watering becomes much more automatic.

Children and teens are like water and will inevitably find those places where parents don't have it all together. If one parent is more inclined than the other to say yes to a request, they will figure that out. Even if the pattern of parental behavior is more complicated, they will, in time, find a weakness.

A last tip on this principle is to create a little code word or signal to help you maintain unity in front of your teen. My wife and I will use the old knee-press-under-the-table at dinner if one of us is talking and the other is trying to signal "Be careful here" or "I'll talk to Mom and we'll let you know." We can then discuss things privately and come out to present our united answer.

6. Change Takes Time and Sustained Effort.

True change is a process that takes time. Parents can help teens make changes by encouraging them through the stages of change, and though you may want to see it done *now*, we know it's not a realistic expectation.

Alcoholism killed James Prochaska's father, so he resolved to find a way to help people break their bad habits. A renowned psychologist at the University of Rhode Island and author of *Changing for Good*, he interviewed people who had been successful "changers." He found a pattern that all self-changers progressed through on their way to recovery from drug use, smoking, overeating, and so on.

a. **Precontemplation:** Essentially, that can be defined as "Problem? What problem?" I don't even know there's a problem yet. We're even beyond awareness at this point.

b. **Contemplation:** Described as "Maybe someday I'll make a change." I'm aware that there's something there, that it's a problem that needs to be addressed, but I'm not ready to tackle it yet.

c. **Preparation:** This can be described as "How am I going to make this change?" We're starting to ask ourselves the question and possibly even take some small steps toward answering it.

d. **Action:** "I'm doing it. One step at a time, I'm doing it."

e. **Maintenance:** "I've been doing this for a while now, and I am working to keep from relapsing."

f. **Termination:** "I am past it and there's no way I would go back."

So consider a few of the changes you are hoping your teen will make and identify which stage you believe he or she is in. Next, identify things that you could do to invite your teen to make the next step. Don't get in the way of his or her natural progression by trying to get him or her to skip ahead. Remember, this takes time. In many cases it took years for your child to become as self-destructive or defiant as he or she has become. Your child has spent some time in a healthy environment in the treatment program to begin to make changes and your job is to solidify those changes at home.

7. Parents Are the Most Powerful Agents of Change.

There is no one living as close to your teen with as much invested in her or his success as you. The love you feel, the sacrifices you've made, the lengths you have gone to in securing help for your teen endows you with power. You may not believe me when I say it, because you've felt so powerless in the past, but it is true that no one can be a more powerful influence on your child's life than you.

Famed Russian author Leo Tolstoy said, "Everyone thinks of changing the world, but no one thinks of changing himself." Focusing on the principles I've outlined in this chapter will increase your ability to stimulate change. Again, by focusing on changing yourselves first, you are going to become more effective parents. You will have a stronger and better relationship with your child and you're going to feel empowered in your parenting, no matter how your teen behaves. It is absolutely the right thing to do and you can sleep at night knowing that you are doing your part by setting an example.

Summary

CHAPTER 12: YOUR TURN: PARENTING—THE NUMBER-ONE THING WITHIN YOUR CONTROL

- As parents we often feel we have no control over our teens. We need to change our focus from their actions to the realm of things we can actually *influence*, not necessarily *change*.

- Parenting principles will cover every situation, because they are principles, not specific answers. By learning and applying principles to parenting situations, you will know how to best handle them.

- Though we mention these principles throughout the book, they are listed together here for your easy reference: parenting leadership is essential to healthy families; nurturing the relationship is a priority; clear expectations encourage consistency and teach values; choice and accountability invite growth; parental unity creates family stability and strength; change takes time and sustained effort; and parents are the most powerful agents of change.

What to Do Now

Take the most recent frustration with your teen and decide which one or two parenting principles address the situation. Reread those pages with this incident in mind. How does it influence your response?

CHAPTER 13

The Game of Life: Over-eighteeners

"I take a very practical view of raising children. I put a sign in each of their rooms: 'Check-out Time is 18 years.'" —ERMA BOMBECK

A s in all transitions, planning and preparing a young person for adulthood can only be accomplished over time. The skills, confidence and internal ethics needed to do well in adulthood can't be poured into a person overnight. Even with years of thoughtful parenting with an eye on this goal, the months and years following transition from home can be full of missteps.

The Gap between Treatment and Independent Living

So what about the case in which we have a young adult who is transitioning out of treatment and has just turned 18? What are the tests that come with this transition? Throughout this book I have encouraged parents to evaluate themselves and the context of home for the re-entry of their teen. As we've discussed, parents are the most powerful agents of change and are in position to be the most influential factor in the long-term success of their teens, apart from the teens themselves, of course. But what about the young adults, the 18-year-olds, who are only going to be home for a couple of months or aren't even coming home to stay before setting up house for themselves?

First, I need to warn that the transition directly to an independent setting such as college is rarely a good idea. Let me paint the picture for you of why this is the case.

Think about the enormous and abrupt changes that teens coming from treatment programs will encounter. They go from a setting where they have understood limitations on what they can and cannot do and when they can do it. They have been surrounded by people who know them intimately. They have had a therapist who has worked with them intensively on a weekly basis and they are leaving a safe environment with opportunities for multiple "do-overs" in their work or relationships. In addition, they have not had their own cell phone, computer, or car. Access to friends outside the treatment setting has been limited to letters and short encounters during home visits. They dream about the day when they will finish treatment and be able to have all these freedoms again.

Then let's say these teens aged out of the program (turned 18) and went directly to an apartment or to on-campus housing. The new environment couldn't be more different from the one these teens just left. Suddenly, they have all the freedoms they were dreaming of. In fact most of those freedoms (cell phone, computer, car) are now potentially essential for their success. They can come and go as they please and on their own time schedule. They have access to drugs, alcohol, sex, gaming and bad friends. They are also faced with the responsibilities of independence—for example, getting to bed on time so they can get up on time, arriving to class or work on time and being coherent enough to succeed in that arena. All of these things require self-leadership, discipline and life skills that these young adults may not have fully developed in the treatment program.

Transition Programs

Transition programs, or "over-18 programs," are popping up all over to address the gap we've just described. It is too big to take on alone. These programs are designed to be an intermediate step between treatment and independent life. Their main focus tends to be on helping young adults gain the necessary independent living skills to be successful on their own. They are encouraged to find their own transportation, enroll in college and hold down a job, yet they return home to an environment that has rules, expectations and ongoing therapy to help them cope and continue to apply the skills they learned in treatment.

Home

Obviously, the other option is for the teen to come home, where you maintain the same goals as a transition program to help the teen launch and become independent. That means you are doing essentially the same thing by helping the teen structure his or her life with school, work, transportation and other life skills. At home the oversight is coming from you rather than a "house" mom or dad. So if the home is going to be an alternative, it needs to be a healthy environment, where parents are not overly enmeshed, have a unified relationship and are not prone to rescuing their teen from challenges, thus stunting their growth.

> If the home is going to be an alternative, it needs to be a healthy environment, where parents are not overly enmeshed, have a unified relationship and are not prone to rescuing their teen from challenges, thus stunting their growth.

The benefit of a transition program is that the staff aren't tied in emotionally; they are there to support but not take over.

This is why all of the skills we have covered in this book are critical for you as a parent considering bringing your young adult home. You need to implement the skills if you want the transition to adulthood to take place with as few stumbles as possible.

Nick

Nick was a student of mine who had been so ruled by his anxiety that when things became difficult for him at school or with a friend, his body would react so violently that he wouldn't be able to keep any food down. When he began to throw up, his mother would whisk him to the hospital for an IV to keep him hydrated. This pattern began with some legitimate health issues, as they often do, and had subsequently taken on a life of its own. The hospitalization would interrupt the situation at home that was causing stress, and he would be rescued from having to deal with it.

At age 17, Nick entered a residential treatment program. During his first three days in the program, the stress built, and sure enough, nothing would stay down. Mom wanted the staff to run him to the hospital because she feared that he would become dehydrated and very sick, but the staff assured her they would keep a close eye on him while providing plenty of fluids and time to settle in further. After three days, he was able to work through the anxiety of the move and subsequently went a full year with no return trips to the hospital. His program staff saw Nick as capable of going through some adversity, learning more about himself and then moving through it to the other side. Their perspective led them to address the problem very differently than Mom had over all those years.

Now, as Nick approached age 18 and was closing in on graduation from the program, the goal was to help him continue toward independence. Yet, as with any old condition, the chance of relapse into dependency was very real. I warned his mom that the old environment and patterns of entitlement and dependence they had co-created were all going to trigger him to resort to old coping mechanisms. We needed to prepare *her* as much as Nick for how he was going to monitor himself when he became anxious that his body would respond by vomiting. This included a step-by-step plan for his mother to remove herself from the equation that was so detrimental and to allow Nick to do more self care. Without successfully breaking the first cycle, ultimate independence would be just a pipe dream.

Failure to Launch

Several years ago my team and I sat down to craft a transition support process for the 18-year-old group that we regularly worked with. The first order of business was to come up with a good name for the program to distinguish it from our aftercare services for younger teens. I primed our team's creativity with a small prize of some sort, which must not have been very exciting because I don't remember the title or the prize. But I do remember the brilliant suggestion I submitted. Mostly in jest, I proposed to call it the "Catapult" program. There were chuckles all around, but they knew it would be attractive to those parents who had a "failure to launch" situation. The catapult action would be seen as a committed launch, decisive and emphatic. I don't know ... I still kind of like it.

So what are the societal factors that are responsible for delayed independence and failure to launch? There are literally dozens of reasons, but I will name just a few:

- Affluence has outright spoiled adults as well as kids. Life requires a fraction of the effort and patience it used to. Grit is a characteristic that is rare. Hence our youth lack the skills and internal fortitude to delay gratification, set goals and put forth the effort to get what they want—starting with their independence.

- Marriage is delayed till the late twenties for multiple reasons. Young people want to be established in their career and home before they commit. The high divorce rates have created a disillusionment with marriage; young people have negative attitudes about their ability to be successful in marriage. This delays what was traditionally one of the great catapult events in life.

- In our society most parents are overprotective, making it difficult for teens to grow up on time. Parents continue to supply food and basement apartments long after young adults have the capacity to provide for themselves.

In spite of the fact that the trends in society lead to longer dependence, people of all ages, starting in childhood, need to feel autonomous and direct their own lives. People who are dependent generally have very poor self-esteem. Even though they like the handouts, there is something inside them that says they don't like being in that situation. Do what it takes to help them make the launch. This launch sequence requires phases, just as sending a space shuttle into the atmosphere does.

As parents, we genuinely want to let go of the reins and watch our children take hold of the responsibilities of adulthood, so in actuality, our goals are aligned with our young adults' at that level. But how we would like to see them live life independently, versus how they choose to live it is going to prove a widening gap. We will cringe at the immature and poor decisions they make, the waste of time, resources and opportunities, or we will be ultra-critical about the people they hang around with. Few of their choices will be as wise as the ones we would make for them, but that is how growth happens: through experience.

Max

Max was in his early 30s, wanting his independence but fearful of taking on all of the responsibility that comes with adult life. The whole family had slipped into a very dysfunctional place, with Dad controlling Max's life because Dad controlled the purse strings. Living with a girlfriend had given Max some sense of maturity and independence. However, Dad was paying for the apartment, the health insurance and some entertainment. While Max would pick up a little job here and there, nothing was ever seen as permanent or fulfilling.

Finally, Max came to a crossroad where his girlfriend was either going to leave him or he was going to have to get married. She didn't want to marry someone who couldn't take care of a family. Mom and Dad were totally at odds; Dad wanted to cut Max off and let him sink or swim, and Mom kept secretly funneling money to him to keep him going. So Max would regularly go to her to keep things afloat.

When I began to help Max, it took everyone coming to the same conclusion, which was that what they had been doing for years would only produce the same results. So we created a six-month launch plan in which, each month, Max's parents paid for fewer and fewer of his living expenses. Essentially, the flow of money would be stopped at the end of that period. Mom and Dad decided they would pay for his medications long-term, but he was responsible for everything else.

Max half-heartedly looked for work until the day he lost his car insurance for not making the payments. Suddenly, he was armed with new motivation—the need for mobility; the choice presented to him was between looking at the bus schedule and looking for more work. I was able to coach him on his résumé, holding him accountable for getting résumés out to apply for possible job opportunities, and for the disciplines of punctuality and not loafing at work. The goal wasn't only to obtain the job but to maintain it.

I continually coached Mom and Dad so that they weren't scared, guilt-ridden or angered into slipping into old patterns of rescuing and enabling Max's irresponsible behavior, or on the other hand, shaming him. Within the six-month period, his confidence had grown, his work ethic had improved and he gained full-time employment. He felt so much more hope and optimism for his future, and he and his girlfriend were later married, resulting in a successful and sustainable launch.

> *"I have learned that if one advances in the direction of his dreams, and endeavors to live the life he has imagined, he will meet with a success unexpected in common hours."* —HENRY DAVID THOREAU

Some young adults have special needs or circumstances that require more support for a longer period of time but often their lack of success in launching is due to the pattern of overinvolvement by their parents starting when they were very young. These are cases where finding a life coach who specializes in helping young adults launch would be valuable.

Tips to Make a Launch Successful

1. Remain accessible

- Call, text or visit periodically (not incessantly).

- Listen: there are going to be exciting and interesting things to hear about, as well as some things that could be warning signs. Remember, listening does not equal agreeing. Ask what your young adult thinks should be done.

- Share experiences or lessons from your own life, when appropriate (first time you moved out, first jobs, burned dinners, etc.).

- Employ consciousness-raising (expressing or explaining things you feel your young adult needs to consider in clear, *short* points—no more than three sentences).

2. Focus on the relationship

- Invite your young adult to participate or continue to participate in family activities (Sunday dinner, birthday celebrations, family vacations, etc.).

- Ask your young adult how things are going and what he or she is learning (don't try to wheedle out information or engage in games of cat and mouse about where your young adult is living).

3. Do *not* enable, fix or rescue.

- Cultivate an attitude of compassion.

- Do not provide money (except in specific situations you can review with your transition coach or therapist).

- Do not provide food (teach basic inexpensive shopping and food prep skills).

- Do not provide a place to do laundry (instead, offer to teach your young adult how to do it, and point out some laundromats in the area).

- Do not purchase clothing, a cell phone, car, and so on for your young adult.

- **Do not accept blame** for your young adult's choices no matter how much he or she insists things are your fault. (You cannot make your young adult happy or sad; he or she must be responsible for his or her own choices now).

  - Repeat the mantra we discussed before. "I'm sorry you feel that way; nevertheless ..."

  - Let your young adult know that though you care about him or her and respect his or her right to make decisions, you don't condone them.

  - Avoid any and all "I told you so's."

4. Things you *should* provide:

- If your young adult requires counseling, provide counseling (but recognize you can't make him or her go).

- If medication is required, provide doctor visits and medication.

- Provide information and instruction on life skills (this includes information on job opportunities, help on interviewing, appropriate help in advancing their education, managing a house, etc.).

- Do provide opportunities and encouragement to discuss plans for success.

- Do express love, concern and confidence in your young adult's ability to succeed.

In spite of the inevitable challenges, point out and celebrate your young adult's successes.

Summary
CHAPTER 13: THE GAME OF LIFE: THE OVEREIGHTEENERS

- A transition from treatment directly to independent living is rarely a good idea, when one considers the enormous and abrupt changes young adults will encounter.

- Over-18 transition programs are popping up to help narrow the gap between the two living situations. Their focus is on the education, money management and job opportunities necessary to move the teen to autonomy, while providing oversight and accountability.

- Home can provide the same oversight as a program would, but as parents, you will need to guard against the enmeshment and rescuing habits that are tempting to fall into when you are watching your own child struggle.

- There are definite do's and don'ts to making a launch successful. Return often to the four tips in this chapter as you redefine your relationship as adult to adult or as your young adult's "independence consultant."

What to Do Now
Make a list of areas in which your young adult will need education. Present it to your young adult with the idea that you are excited about his or her upcoming independence and would like to offer support in achieving that independence as soon as your young adult proves ready for it.

CHAPTER 14

We've Got a Winner: The Role of Aftercare In Long-Term Success

"Press forward. Do not stop, do not linger in your journey, but strive for the mark set before you." —George Whitefield

At the beginning of this book, I told you that I would give you the best of what we have learned in nearly a decade of working inside the homes of hundreds of families. I have given you research, stories, step-by-steps, templates, metaphors, warnings and encouragement, and you have just about completed your self-directed education through this book. Your journey from the crises that led to treatment, and the treatment process itself has been long and arduous. Your teen's progress has been hard won with the help of expert guides combined with specialized settings where change is easier to nurture. Now, as you consider the transition home, you instinctively understand how important and difficult this will be.

Why Aftercare?

Even with a good plan, which you should have after reading this book, most teens and families benefit from having help to implement the plan and support them through the challenges. They realize what they are up against. The drag of old familiar contexts, relationships, triggers and temptations can be devastating to the commitments, goals and momentum prior to leaving treatment. Former heavyweight boxing champ Mike Tyson isn't exactly a world-class example of good judgment, but he did say something quite insightful that certainly applies here, "Everybody has a plan until they get hit." Having the right support after treatment is often the difference between success and failure. The outcome research referred to in chapter one is unquestioningly clear about the importance of good aftercare for long-term success. Speak to your program therapist and/or your referring professional and talk about next steps and what type of support would be best for your circumstances, then find help from someone who has a model and expertise around transition.

My good friend Dr. Ken Newell is one of the few therapists who have worked with teens throughout the continuum of care. From in-home intervention to wilderness, residential, therapeutic boarding school and transition, he has some solid counsel for parents regarding long-term success and the place of aftercare support.

> "After consulting with therapists and educational consultants with decades of experience, we seem to agree on this one thing: the key factor in success is if the parents/family make the

changes necessary to meet their teen where they are at emotionally when they return home. If they do not, they will still be operating from the place their teen was in before treatment.

When testing begins, parents may think everything was a huge waste and the teens haven't changed. The bigger truth is that the teen is not the same. That teen may appear to get into the same situations, but now he or she possesses the tools and skills to work out of them. The question to success now becomes, do the parents now possess the new skills and tools to work their teen out of the bad situation? If not, the family system will quickly resort to the old dysfunctional ways of interacting and the cycle will resume where it left off. Parents must learn new skills, internalize them and refuse to give up the first time they are tested. But this is extremely challenging. My observation is that most families who successfully reunite, had parents and teens who committed to using their new skills, and who had expert support to help them continue to do so when things became difficult."

Along with the research regarding the importance of aftercare, here are comments from a few of our families.

All our prayers were answered, a hundred times over—the right people at the right time in the right place. God makes all things possible. Our family was like Sleeping Beauty or a cat in a tree: frozen in time and afraid to move. We're moving on now. I can't believe the changes in my husband, our daughter and hopefully myself. We have truly undertaken to understand and apply what we've learned. Our coach and our home team have been just the right people to carry us forward at home. It was exactly the support I was hoping for. You helped us get rid of the chaos and uncertainty of daily life so we could deal with periodic moments of being in the box. Then you encouraged us, helping us deal with it and patting us on the back when we succeeded. WOW! Crash course in what we needed all along. Thanks again. —PARENT (CALIFORNIA)

A father shared:

I don't think there is any question that a kid shouldn't be sent home from a program without aftercare support. I just think it should be incorporated into the program because I think the experiences are so intense and there is so much heavy expectation and anticipation of what that homecoming is going to be like. You just need somebody to help you facilitate through it. We were so full of anticipation when Evan was coming home and literally within a day it was like he had never been away. It was just really shocking and scary. I don't know what would have happened if our coach hadn't arrived when she did. —PARENT (IDAHO)

Here's what a mother had to say:

Aftercare is an exceptional part of our son's journey as well as that of our family's. It complemented our son's therapeutic program to perfection. The privilege of having an expert observe our interactions and comment on the spot was exactly what we needed: direct, honest, constructive feedback, a better understanding of our challenges, and a plan. Strictly speaking the return on investment was immediate, concrete and visible. Our level of awareness collectively grew and that in itself enabled the four of us to modify many behavior patterns.

For sure, it is not magic. We still have challenges to face, our son in particular, but we are now better equipped to face life as parents and teenagers. More importantly when needed, we know who to call. For all these reasons, and many others, our coach helped us develop perspective. And that gave us hope. Hope for our son. In addition, because of the changes we have all made, the love and humor is back in our family again—best remedy in the world!

In short, transition work was the best thing we did for our family. Do not hesitate. It is the right thing to do. —PARENT (TAIPEI, TAIWAN)

What Success Looks Like

The Stephens family was one of our first, before we had successfully navigated through all the phases of transition and it was tough. Picture a son returning from treatment and within the week he was drinking and testing in huge ways. In the most recent act of rebellion, his anger had gotten so out of control that he had taken his hockey stick to the living room mantel. He then took the broken stick and threatened his mother with it. The police were called, and the parents were horrified and frozen in fear. In the beginning I had to support not only the family but their coach as well, with my belief in the power of what we were doing. To be truthful, even I had periods of doubt. We were new at this, and this was the first family I had seen go through the wringer at this level. We had no other professional organization doing this work in our niche whose lead we could follow. Their coach and I sat in counsel with them to keep them calm and focused on the structure we had set in place. In private, their coach and I looked at each other and said "Are we doing the right thing? Can they really handle this?" We knew that these were true principles we were teaching but would they work for this family? We were greatly concerned and considered having them change course. Ultimately, we bolstered our confidence in the principles and in the family and encouraged them to continue. The expression of our belief in the power of these principles was critical for the Stephens family to push through and achieve the peace and confidence they were seeking.

One of the great joys in my work is hearing from former clients. The last time we heard from the Stephens, their son was trying to decide if he should attend law school at his father's alma mater, or choose a school in Colorado. The relationships were strong between parents and son and between the son and their daughter. They had come through the treatment and transition experiences with that confidence born of a trial imbued with action, faith and love.

CONCLUSION

If you need to borrow my faith in your abilities for a time, by all means do it. It's what I'm here for. I have no doubt you will emerge from this journey down your life's river more experienced, wise and appreciative of what your family has gained.

Family life is meant to provide both growth and joy while we are on the earth. You have been given gifts to utilize as you deliberately work at keeping your family connected and strong. I know you will be helped and find success as you focus on winning the day.

I wish you and your family all of the love, healing and joy that you deserve.

REFERENCES

Burns, B. J., Hoagwood, K., & Mrazek, P. J. (1999). Effective treatment for mental disorders in children and adolescents. *Clinical Child and Family Review, 2,* 199–254.

Chapman, Gary D. (2009), *The Five Love Languages: The Secret to Love That Lasts,* Northfield Publishing.

Charles, G., & McIntyre, S. (1990). *The best of care: Recommendations for the future of residential services for troubled and troubling young people in Canada.* Ottawa, ON: Canadian Child Welfare Association.

Clark, Timothy, R. (2012), *The Employee Management Mindset: The Six Drivers for Tapping into the Hidden Potential of Everyone in Your Company,* McGraw Hill Companies, Inc.

Covey, Stephen R. (2004), *Seven Habits of Highly Effective People,* Free Press.

DuBois, D.L., Holloway, B.E., Valentine, J.C., Cooper, H. (2002), "Effectiveness of Mentoring Programs for Youth: A Meta-analytic Review." *American Journal of Community Psychology* 30, no. 2: 157-197.

DuBois, D. L. and N. Silverthorne (2005), "Characteristics of Natural Mentoring Relationships and Adolescent Adjustment: Evidence from a National Study," *Journal of Primary Prevention* 26: 69–92.

DuBois, D. L., N. Portillo, J. E. Rhodes, N. Silverthorne, and J. C. Valentine (2011), "How Effective Are Mentoring Programs for Youth? A Systematic Assessment of the Evidence," *Psychological Science in the Public Interest* 12: 57–91.

Ensher, Ellen and Susan Murphy (2005), *Power Mentoring: How Successful Mentors and Protégés Get the Most out of Their Relationships*, Josey Bass.

Frensch, K. M., & Cameron, G. (2002). "Treatment of choice or a last resort? A review of residential mental health placements for children and youth." *Child and Youth Care Forum,* 31, 307–339.

Hair, H. (2005), "Outcomes for Children and Adolescents after Residential Treatment: A Review of Research from 1993 to 2003," *Journal of Child and Family Studies* 14, no. 4: 551–575.

Heath, D. (2005), *Growing More Mature,* Philadelphia: Conrow.

Lambert, M. J. (1992). Implications of outcome research for psychotherapy integration. IN J.C. Norcross & M.R. Goldstein (Eds.). *Handbook of Psychotherapy Integration* (pp. 94-129). New York: Basic Books.

Maushart, Susan (2010), *The Winter of Our Disconnect: How Three Totally Wired Teenagers (and a Mother Who Slept with Her iPhone) Pulled the Plug on Their Technology and Lived to Tell the Tale*, Jeremy P. Tarcher/Penguin, 185.

Ministry of Community and Social Services (1978, September). Children's residential care facilities: *Proposed standards and guidelines.* Government of Ontario: Children's Services Division.

Moretti, Marlene M. and Maya Peled (2004), "Adolescent-Parent Attachment: Bonds That Support Healthy Development," *Pediatric Child Health* 9, no. 8 (October): 551–555; http://www.ncbi.nlm. nih.gov/pmc/articles/PMC2724162/

Pink, Daniel H. (2009), *Drive: The Surprising Truth about What Motivates Us,* Riverhead Books.

Prochaska, James John Norcross and Carlo DiClemente (1994), *Changing for Good,* William Morrow.

Rae-Grant, Q., & Moffat, P. J. (1971). "Children in Canada— residential care." Toronto: The Canadian Mental Health Association.

Sunseri, Paul A. (2004), "Family Functioning and Residential Treatment Outcome." *Journal of Residential Treatment for Children and Youth* 22, no. 1: 33–53.

Taylor, D. A., & Alpert, S. W. (1973). "Continuity and support following residential treatment." New York: Child Welfare League of America.

Wampold, B. E. (2001). "The great psychotherapy debate: models, methods and findings." Hahwah, NJ: Erlbaum.

Zimmerman, M. A., J. B. Bingenheimer, and D. E. Behrendt (2005), "Natural mentoring relationships," in *Handbook of Youth Mentoring,* ed. D. L. DuBois and M. L. Karcher, 143–159, Thousand Oaks, CA: Sage Publications, Inc.

INDEX

Additional *Not by Chance* Resources

For more ideas to boost your
son or daughter's treatment success visit
www.NotbyChance.com

Featuring

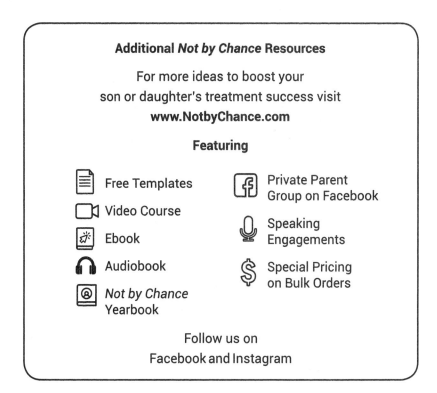

Free Templates

Video Course

Ebook

Audiobook

Not by Chance
Yearbook

Private Parent
Group on Facebook

Speaking
Engagements

Special Pricing
on Bulk Orders

Follow us on
Facebook and Instagram

Homeward Bound

To learn more about world-class coaching services
no matter where you call home, visit

www.HomewardBound.com

For 15 years this team of Master's and
Ph.D. level coaches have helped young
people and their families with

Parent Coaching

Early Intervention

Transition Planning

Transition Services

Reach out at 801-768-1441

For anyone who wants better relationships and success at the office and at home.

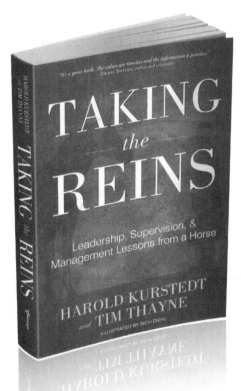

Kurstedt and Thayne team up to deliver a book that encourages management techniques focused on relationships, supervision based on realistic expectations, and leadership through recognition of the strengths of others.

"I have never been a fan of leadership books until reading Taking the Reins. *The plain spoken principles and stories resonate with the reader allowing retention of the key lessons. A must read for leaders that want to create followership."*

—DONALD E. STONE, JR., PE, Chief Executive Officer, Dewberry

"Keeps the reader engaged, and even entertained, so the material is understandable, believable and valuable. With the clever use of horse tales and horse sense, the concepts are presented and explained in a way that will stick with me like no other work."

—MIKE LEINBACH, Space Shuttle Launch Director